Alaska Travel Guide 2025

Your Essential Planner for Fairbanks, the Northern Lights, National Parks, and Offbeat Discoveries

Wyatt Caleb

Copyright © 2025 Wyatt Caleb

All rights reserved.

No part of this book may be reproduced, distributed, or transmitted in any form or by any means, including photocopying, recording, or other electronic or mechanical methods, without the prior written permission of the publisher, except in the case of brief quotations embodied in critical reviews and certain other noncommercial uses permitted by copyright law.

Table of Contents

INTRODUCTION 6
MAP OF ALASKA 9
WELCOME TO ALASKA 10
CHAPTER 1: GETTING STARTED 12
Why Alaska? 12
Getting Around 14
Health & Safe Travel 17
12 Must-Visit Historical Sites 19
Packing Checklist for Alaska 23
Budget Planning for Your Trip 26
LGBTIQ+ Travelers 28
10 Do's and Don'ts in Alaska 29
Best Times to Visit 31
Essential Travel Tips for First-Timers 32
CHAPTER 2: ANCHORAGE 34
When to Visit 34
Top Attractions in Anchorage 35
Outdoor Activities and Day Trips 37
Where to Stay and Eat 39
CHAPTER 3: FAIRBANKS 41
Exploring Fairbanks' History and Culture 41
Northern Lights Viewing 42
Hot Springs, Wildlife, and Unique Experiences 44
CHAPTER 4: GLACIERS, FJORDS, AND COASTAL WONDERS 45
Cruising the Inside Passage 45
Highlights of Juneau, Ketchikan, Petersburg, Wrangell, and Sitka 46
Whale Watching and Glacier Adventures 51
CHAPTER 5: DENALI NATIONAL PARK AND BEYOND 55
Trails, Wildlife, and Scenic Drives 55
Camping and Lodging Options 61

Off-the-Beaten-Path Adventures   65
CHAPTER 6: THE ARCTIC CIRCLE AND REMOTE ALASKA   69
Crossing the Arctic Circle   69
Barrow (Utqiaġvik) and Nome   72
Indigenous Culture and Traditions   76
CHAPTER 7: WILDLIFE ENCOUNTERS AND NATURE EXPLORATION   79
Alaska's Big Five   79
Birdwatching and Marine Life   84
Responsible Wildlife Viewing Tips   87
CHAPTER 8: NOME AND THE ARCTIC   90
When to Visit   90
Top Attractions   93
Where to Eat and Stay   100
CHAPTER 9: OFF-THE-GRID ESCAPES AND OUTDOOR ADVENTURES   106
Backcountry Hiking and Camping   106
Kayaking, Fishing, and Dog Sledding   109
Staying Safe in the Wilderness   112
CHAPTER 10: PRACTICAL TRAVEL TIPS AND RESOURCES   114
Packing for Alaska   114
Flights, Ferries, and Road Trips   116
Budgeting and Planning Your Trip   120
CONCLUSION   123
BONUS   125
Detailed Maps of Key Regions   125
Itineraries for Every Traveler (3-Day, 7-Day, and 14-Day Plans)   129
12 Must-Try Alaskan Dishes and Where to Find Them   135
ABOUT THE AUTHOR   139

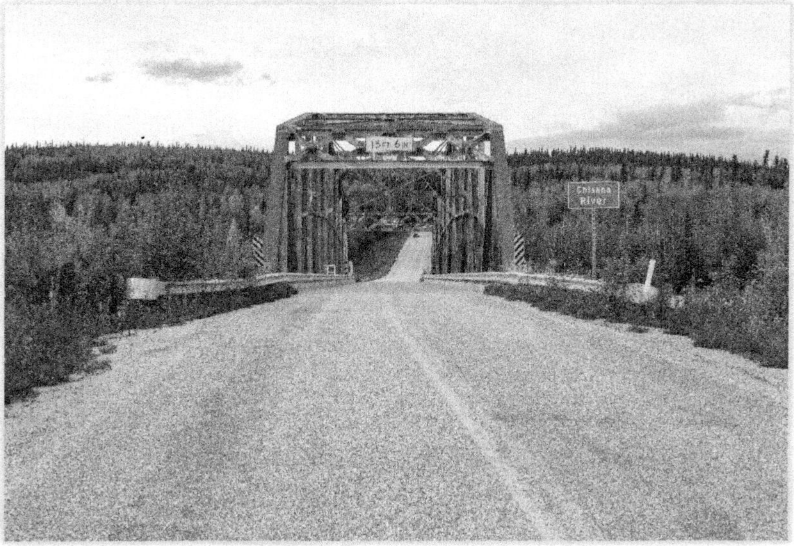
15 FT 6 IN
Chisana River

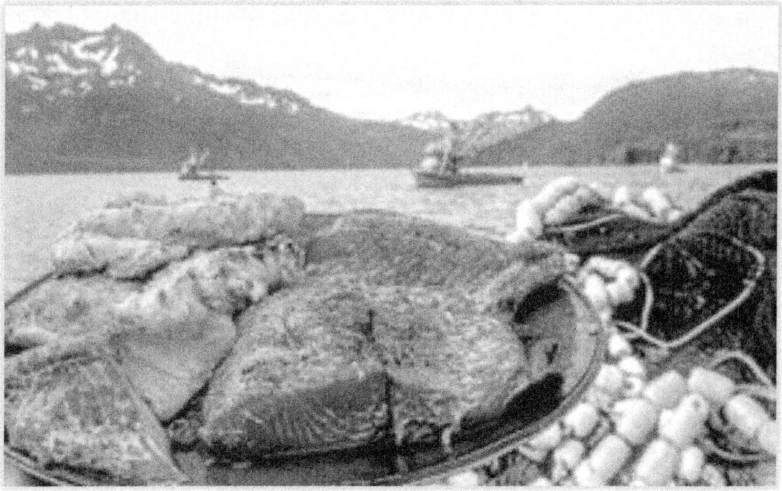

Introduction

I know you're either planning a trip to Alaska or preparing to explore its breathtaking landscapes, and you want to make sure you don't miss out on the incredible experiences this destination has to offer. That's why you've chosen this guide—great decision! Welcome, and let me share a bit about my visit to Alaska in 2023 and why I believe it's a place you absolutely must experience in 2025.

During my last trip, I was reminded of how extraordinary Alaska truly is. It's a land where nature feels boundless and untamed. The towering mountains, vast forests, and glistening glaciers create a setting that's unlike anywhere else. One of the most unforgettable moments for me was standing in Denali National Park, gazing at the awe-inspiring Denali peak. The quiet of the park, broken only by the distant sounds of wildlife, was a moment of pure serenity. I was even lucky enough to spot a grizzly bear from a safe distance—an encounter that left me in awe of Alaska's raw beauty.

Another highlight was visiting Glacier Bay. Watching enormous chunks of ice break off glaciers and crash into the water was mesmerizing. The sound of the ice cracking and falling was like a low, powerful rumble, and the sheer size of the glaciers was humbling. I also had the chance to kayak in Resurrection Bay, paddling alongside playful sea otters and catching a glimpse of a humpback whale breaching in the distance. These moments made me feel deeply connected to the wild.

Alaska isn't just about its natural wonders—it's also about its rich culture and welcoming people. In Fairbanks, I explored Alaska's Native heritage and traditions, which gave me a deeper understanding of the region's history. And the food? Freshly caught salmon and king crab legs straight from Alaskan waters are culinary experiences you won't forget.

What makes Alaska truly special is how it offers something for everyone. Whether you're chasing the Northern Lights, hiking through untouched wilderness, or simply enjoying the beauty of the midnight sun, Alaska leaves a lasting impression. It's not just a trip—it's an experience that stays with you forever.

As you plan your adventure, this guide is here to help you make the most of your time in Alaska. Trust me, you're about to embark on an unforgettable journey.

Map of Alaska

Welcome to Alaska

Welcome to Alaska, a land of breathtaking beauty, untamed wilderness, and unforgettable adventures. Known as the Last Frontier, Alaska captivates travelers from across the globe with its unique landscapes and unparalleled experiences. Whether you're drawn to its towering mountains, expansive glaciers, or incredible wildlife, Alaska offers something special for every visitor.

One of the first things you'll notice about Alaska is its immense size. Spanning over 663,000 square miles, it's the largest state in the U.S., yet one of the least populated. This means you'll encounter vast open spaces, untouched natural beauty, and a sense of solitude that's hard to find elsewhere. From the vibrant city life of Anchorage to the remote serenity of the Arctic Circle, Alaska is a destination where adventure and tranquility exist side by side.

The state's natural wonders are truly one of a kind. Alaska is home to iconic national parks like Denali National Park, where North America's tallest peak dominates the skyline, and Glacier Bay, where colossal glaciers meet the ocean. The Northern Lights, a dazzling display of colors in the night sky, is another bucket-list experience that draws visitors year-round. Whether you're hiking through dense forests, cruising along icy fjords, or simply soaking in the views, Alaska's landscapes will leave you speechless.

Beyond its scenery, Alaska is about the experiences it offers. Picture yourself watching a grizzly bear catch salmon in a rushing river, kayaking alongside playful sea otters, or learning about the traditions of Alaska's Native communities. The state's culture is as diverse as its geography, blending Indigenous heritage, Russian influences, and modern American life into a fascinating tapestry.

For outdoor enthusiasts, Alaska is an unmatched playground. From fishing in Sitka Bay and hiking the Kenai Peninsula to dog sledding in Fairbanks, there's no shortage of activities to fuel your sense of adventure. And for food lovers, Alaska's fresh seafood—like wild salmon, halibut, and king crab—is a culinary highlight you won't want to miss.

As you prepare for your journey, remember that Alaska is more than just a destination—it's an experience that will stay with you forever. Welcome to a place where nature takes center stage, and every moment is an adventure waiting to unfold.

Chapter 1: Getting Started

Why Alaska?

Alaska is more than just a destination—it's an experience unlike any other. Known as the Last Frontier, it's a land of contrasts, where vast wilderness meets a rich cultural history, and adventure awaits at every turn. Whether you're captivated by its stunning landscapes, fascinated by its incredible wildlife, or eager to immerse yourself in a way of life far removed from the ordinary, Alaska offers something for everyone.

One of Alaska's most remarkable features is its natural beauty. The state boasts towering mountains, sprawling glaciers, and endless forests that stretch beyond the horizon. Denali, the tallest peak in North America, stands as a testament to Alaska's grandeur, while Glacier Bay and Kenai Fjords highlight the raw power and elegance of ice and water. These landscapes are not just picturesque—they're dynamic, constantly shifting with the seasons and offering new wonders to explore with every visit.

Alaska's wildlife is another reason it stands out as a travel destination. Few places on Earth provide such incredible opportunities to observe animals in their natural habitats. From grizzly bears fishing for salmon in rivers to bald eagles soaring overhead, Alaska is a haven for wildlife enthusiasts. Whale watching in the Inside Passage, spotting moose along quiet trails, or seeing caribou roam the tundra are just a few of the unforgettable encounters you can experience.

The state's cultural heritage is equally captivating. Alaska is home to vibrant Native communities that have lived in harmony with the land for thousands of years. Visitors can explore their traditions, art, and history through cultural centers, museums, and local events. Additionally, remnants of Russian influence from Alaska's colonial past add another layer of historical intrigue.

For those seeking adventure, Alaska is unmatched. Whether you're hiking in Denali National Park, kayaking through Prince William Sound, or dog sledding across snowy terrain, the opportunities for outdoor exploration are endless. Even a simple drive along Alaska's scenic highways feels like an adventure, with every turn revealing breathtaking views and hidden treasures.

Alaska is a place where nature, culture, and adventure blend seamlessly. It's a destination that pushes you to step outside your comfort zone, rewards you with unforgettable experiences, and leaves you yearning to return. Alaska isn't just a place to visit—it's a place to truly experience.

Getting Around

Alaska's vast size and rugged terrain make transportation a critical part of trip planning. With limited road networks and many remote destinations, getting around often requires a combination of travel methods. Whether you're flying between cities, cruising along the coast, or driving scenic highways, each option provides a unique way to experience Alaska's stunning landscapes.

Flights

Flying is the fastest and most practical way to cover Alaska's immense distances, especially when traveling between major cities or reaching remote areas. Airlines like Alaska Airlines and Ravn Alaska offer regular flights connecting Anchorage, Fairbanks, Juneau, and smaller towns such as Ketchikan, Sitka, and Kodiak. For instance, a one-way flight from Anchorage to Juneau (approximately

850 miles or 1,368 km) typically costs between $150 and $300, depending on the season. For remote destinations, bush planes and air taxis are essential. These smaller aircraft provide access to places like the Arctic Circle, national parks, and isolated villages. Prices for bush flights start at around $200 for short trips and increase for longer or chartered flights. Be aware that weather conditions can cause delays, so it's wise to allow flexibility in your schedule.

Ferries

The Alaska Marine Highway System (AMHS) offers a scenic and unique way to explore Alaska's coastal regions. Ferries connect towns along the Inside Passage, Prince William Sound, and beyond, providing breathtaking views of glaciers, fjords, and marine wildlife. A one-way ferry ride from Juneau to Sitka (14 hours, 155 miles or 249 km) costs around $50–$70 per passenger, with an additional $100–$150 for vehicles. Cabins are available for longer trips, starting at $50 per night. Ferries are ideal for travelers bringing cars or RVs while enjoying the coastal scenery. However, schedules can be limited, especially during the off-season, so booking in advance is essential.

Trains

The Alaska Railroad is a popular choice for travelers seeking a comfortable and scenic way to explore the state. Notable routes include the Denali Star (Anchorage to Fairbanks, 356 miles or 573 km) and the Coastal Classic (Anchorage to Seward, 114 miles or 183 km). Ticket prices range from $100 to $250 per person, depending on the route and class. For a premium experience, GoldStar Service offers glass-domed cars, outdoor viewing platforms, and meals, with prices starting at $300. Train travel is perfect for those who want to relax and enjoy Alaska's breathtaking landscapes without the stress of driving.

Road Trips

Driving is one of the best ways to explore Alaska's diverse landscapes at your own pace. The state's highway system includes some of the most scenic routes in the world, such as the Seward Highway (127 miles or 204 km) and the Parks Highway (323 miles or 520 km). Car rentals in Anchorage typically cost $50–$100 per day, while RV rentals range from $150 to $300 per day. Gas prices in Alaska are higher than the national average, usually around $4–$5 per gallon. On remote routes like the Dalton

Highway (414 miles or 666 km from Fairbanks to Prudhoe Bay), be prepared for long stretches without services. Always carry extra fuel, food, water, and emergency supplies.

Tips for Remote Areas

Traveling in Alaska's remote regions requires careful preparation. Cell service is often limited or nonexistent, so download offline maps or carry a physical map. Weather conditions can change rapidly, so check forecasts and road conditions before heading out. If traveling to isolated areas, inform someone of your itinerary and expected return time. For added safety, consider renting a satellite phone or GPS device. Always pack layers and weather-appropriate gear, as conditions can shift unexpectedly, even during summer.

Health & Safe Travel

Traveling in Alaska is an unforgettable experience, but its rugged terrain and unpredictable weather demand careful planning to ensure your trip is both safe and enjoyable. Here are some practical health and safety tips to help you navigate Alaska's unique environment.

Weather Preparedness

Alaska's weather is highly unpredictable, even during the summer months. Daytime temperatures in summer typically range from 50°F to 70°F (10°C to 21°C), but evenings can be much cooler, and rain is frequent, especially in coastal areas like Juneau and Ketchikan. In winter, temperatures in places like Fairbanks can drop to -40°F (-40°C) or lower. Always dress in layers, including a waterproof outer layer, and pack essentials such as gloves, hats, and sturdy, insulated boots. A high-quality rain jacket is essential for staying dry in Alaska's often wet conditions.

Wildlife Safety

Alaska's wildlife is one of its biggest draws, but encounters with animals like bears and moose can be dangerous if not handled properly. When hiking, always carry bear spray, which can be purchased for $30–$50 at outdoor stores in cities like Anchorage or Fairbanks, and ensure you know how to use it. Make noise while on trails to avoid surprising wildlife, and never approach or feed animals. If you're camping, store all food in bear-proof containers, which can often be rented for $5–$10 per day at national parks or outdoor gear shops.

Emergency Resources

Cell service is limited or nonexistent in many remote areas of Alaska, so it's important to carry a physical map or download offline maps before heading out. For backcountry adventures, consider renting a satellite phone or GPS device, which typically costs $15–$20 per day. Always inform someone of your itinerary and expected return time before venturing into isolated areas. In case of emergencies, Alaska's State Troopers and search-and-rescue teams are well-trained, but response times may be delayed in remote regions.

12 Must-Visit Historical Sites

Alaska's history is as expansive and captivating as its landscapes. From its Indigenous roots to Russian colonization, the Gold Rush, and its strategic importance during World War II, the state is home to numerous historical sites that tell the story of its rich and diverse past. Here are 12 must-visit historical locations that offer a deeper understanding of Alaska's heritage.

1. **Sitka National Historical Park**
   Located in Sitka, this park commemorates the 1804 Battle of Sitka between the Tlingit people and Russian settlers. Visitors can walk the Totem Trail, featuring intricately carved totem poles, and learn about Tlingit culture. Entry is free, and the park is a short distance from downtown Sitka.

2. **Klondike Gold Rush National Historical Park**
   Situated in Skagway, this park highlights the 1898 Gold Rush that brought thousands of prospectors to Alaska. Explore restored buildings in the historic district and hike the famous Chilkoot Trail. Entry to the visitor center is free, while guided tours and trail permits cost $10–$20.

3. **Alaska Native Heritage Center**
   Located in Anchorage, this center celebrates the traditions of Alaska's 11 major Native groups. Visitors can explore traditional dwellings, watch cultural performances, and join workshops. Admission is $29.95 for adults and $19.95 for children.

4. **Kennicott Mine and Ghost Town**
   Nestled in Wrangell-St. Elias National Park, this

abandoned copper mining town offers a glimpse into Alaska's industrial history. Guided tours of the mill building cost around $30, and the site is accessible via a 60-mile gravel road from Chitina.

5. **Russian Bishop's House**
Located in Sitka, this 19th-century building is one of the last remaining examples of Russian colonial architecture in North America. Tours cost $8 per person and provide insight into the Russian Orthodox Church's influence in Alaska.

6. **Totem Bight State Historical Park**
Near Ketchikan, this park features 14 restored totem poles and a replica clan house. Admission is free, and the park is located about 10 miles (16 km) from downtown Ketchikan, accessible by car or bus.

7. **Baranof Castle Hill State Historic Site**
Located in Sitka, this site marks the location where Alaska was officially transferred from Russia to the United States in 1867. The hill offers panoramic views of Sitka Sound, and entry is free.

8. **Crow Creek Mine**

   Near Girdwood, this historic gold mine allows visitors to pan for gold and explore original mining buildings. Admission is $10, and gold panning experiences start at $25. The site is about 40 miles (64 km) southeast of Anchorage.

9. **Fort William H. Seward**
   Located in Haines, this former military post was established during the Klondike Gold Rush to maintain order. Today, it features art galleries, shops, and museums. Entry is free, and it's a short walk from the Haines ferry terminal.

10. **Oscar Anderson House Museum**
    This historic home in Anchorage, built in 1915, offers a glimpse into early 20th-century life in Alaska. Guided tours cost $10 per person, and the house is located in Elderberry Park near downtown Anchorage.

11. **Independence Mine State Historical Park**
    Located in the Hatcher Pass area, this site preserves the remains of a 1930s gold mining operation. Visitors can explore the buildings and learn about

the lives of miners. Admission is $5 per vehicle, and the park is about 60 miles (97 km) north of Anchorage.

12. **Dutch Harbor Naval Operating Base and Fort Mears**

    Located in Unalaska, this World War II site played a key role in defending Alaska from Japanese attacks. Visitors can explore remnants of bunkers and gun emplacements. Access is free, but reaching Unalaska requires a flight from Anchorage.

Packing Checklist for Alaska

Packing for Alaska requires thoughtful preparation due to its unpredictable weather and the variety of activities available. Whether you're hiking in Denali, spotting wildlife in Kenai Fjords, or exploring Anchorage, having the right gear is essential. Here's a practical checklist tailored to Alaska's seasons and activities:

Year-Round Essentials

- **Layered Clothing**: Pack base layers ($30–$60), mid-layers like fleece jackets ($50–$100), and waterproof outer layers ($100–$200) to adapt to Alaska's changing weather.

- **Sturdy Footwear**: Waterproof hiking boots ($100–$200) for outdoor adventures and comfortable walking shoes for city exploration.

- **Reusable Water Bottle**: Insulated bottles ($20–$40) to keep beverages hot or cold.

- **Binoculars**: A must for wildlife viewing, with prices starting at $50.

- **Backpack**: A daypack ($30–$70) for carrying essentials during hikes or day trips.

- **Bug Spray and Sunscreen**: Mosquitoes are common in summer, and sunscreen is necessary year-round to protect against UV rays.

Seasonal Additions

- **Summer (June–August)**:
    - Lightweight rain jacket ($50–$100) for unexpected showers.
    - Quick-dry clothing for activities like kayaking or fishing.

- Bug net ($10–$20) for mosquito-heavy areas.

- **Fall (September–November)**:
  - Insulated jacket ($100–$200) for cooler evenings.
  - Wool socks ($10–$20 per pair) to keep your feet warm.

- **Winter (December–February)**:
  - Heavy down coat ($150–$300) for freezing temperatures.
  - Thermal gloves and hats ($20–$50 each).
  - Snow boots with excellent traction ($100–$200).

- **Spring (March–May)**:
  - Waterproof hiking pants ($50–$100) for muddy trails.
  - Light gloves and a beanie for chilly mornings.

Activity-Specific Gear

- **Hiking**: Trekking poles ($30–$80) for uneven terrain and a compact first-aid kit ($15–$30).

- **Wildlife Viewing**: A camera with a zoom lens ($300+) and a wildlife guidebook ($10–$20) to identify animals.

- **City Exploration**: Casual layers and comfortable walking shoes for exploring urban areas like Anchorage or Fairbanks.

Budget Planning for Your Trip

When organizing a trip to Alaska, it's essential to budget wisely, as costs can escalate quickly due to the state's remote nature and distinctive attractions. Typically, mid-range accommodations in cities like Anchorage and Fairbanks range from $100 to $200 per night. In contrast, more secluded lodges can be priced between $300 and $600 per night. For those looking to save, hostels and campgrounds offer more economical options, usually costing between $20 and $50 per night.

Engaging in activities like glacier cruises or wildlife excursions usually falls within the $100 to $250 range per person, while premium experiences, such as flightseeing tours, can range from $300 to $500. To keep expenses down, consider traveling during the shoulder seasons (May or September) when prices are often lower, and be sure to book activities ahead of time to take advantage of any available discounts.

Transportation is another considerable expense to factor in. Car rentals typically cost between $50 and $100 per day, and gas prices in Alaska tend to exceed the national average, generally hovering around $4 to $5 per gallon. If you opt for the Alaska Marine Highway ferries, fares will vary from $50 to $150 per person based on the route and distance.

To help manage food expenses, consider grocery shopping and cooking your own meals, as dining out can range from $15 to $30 per meal. With thoughtful planning and savvy choices, you can explore Alaska's stunning landscapes and adventures without going over budget.

LGBTIQ+ Travelers

Alaska is a welcoming destination for LGBTIQ+ travelers, offering inclusive places and resources to ensure a safe and enjoyable experience. In Anchorage, the largest city in the state, you can find LGBTQ-friendly venues like Mad Myrna's, a popular bar known for its drag shows and vibrant events. Talkeetna, a quirky and charming town located approximately 115 miles (185 km) north of Anchorage, is also renowned for its lively arts community and open-minded atmosphere.

While public displays of affection are typically accepted in urban settings, they might draw attention in more rural areas. It's wise to remain aware of your surroundings and consider reaching out to local LGBTQ+ organizations or groups for guidance, support, and recommendations throughout your visit.

10 Do's and Don'ts in Alaska

10 Important Do's and Don'ts in Alaska

Do's

1. **Honor Indigenous Cultures**: Alaska is home to over 200 Indigenous tribes. Take the time to learn about their traditions and visit cultural sites like the Alaska Native Heritage Center in Anchorage (admission: $29.95 for adults).

2. **Maintain a Safe Distance from Wildlife**: Keep at least 300 feet (91 meters) away from bears and 100 yards (91 meters) from marine mammals. Carry bear spray (costing around $40 to $50) when hiking.

3. **Dress in Layers**: The weather in Alaska can change rapidly. Bring waterproof jackets, insulated clothing, and durable boots suitable for all seasons.

4. **Adhere to Leave No Trace Principles**: Properly dispose of waste, stay on designated trails, and avoid disturbing wildlife habitats.

5. **Prepare for Limited Cell Service**: In remote locations, it's wise to have a physical map handy or download offline maps for navigation.

Don'ts

1. **Avoid Feeding Wildlife**: Feeding animals disrupts their natural behaviors and can pose dangers to both wildlife and humans.

2. **Don't Underestimate Weather Conditions**: Even during summer, temperatures in certain areas can drop below freezing. Always be prepared for changing weather.

3. **Follow Local Regulations**: Adhere to rules regarding fishing, hunting, and camping to avoid penalties.

4. **Do Not Approach Glaciers Carelessly**: Glaciers can calve unexpectedly. Always participate in guided tours for your safety.

5. **Secure Your Food Properly**: Use bear-proof containers when camping to prevent attracting wildlife.

Best Times to Visit

The ideal time to visit Alaska varies based on your interests and the experiences you wish to have. **Summer** (from June to August) is the most favored season, featuring long days, mild temperatures ranging from 50°F to 70°F (10°C to 21°C), and prime opportunities for activities such as hiking, wildlife observation, and fishing. This season is also optimal for cruises and visiting national parks like Denali and Kenai Fjords. However, it is also the busiest and priciest time, with accommodation rates typically between 150and150 and 150and300 per night in popular areas.

The **shoulder seasons** (May and September) are perfect for those on a budget. May presents excellent birdwatching and blooming wildflowers, while September showcases vibrant fall foliage and provides chances to witness the Northern Lights in Fairbanks. During these months, temperatures hover around 40°F to 60°F (4°C to 15°C), and prices for lodging and tours tend to be more affordable.

Winter (from October to April) caters to Northern Lights enthusiasts and offers winter sports such as dog sledding and skiing. In Fairbanks, temperatures can plummet to -40°F (-40°C), so be sure to pack appropriately. Winter activities are generally less expensive, with smaller crowds and unique experiences like the Iditarod sled dog race.

Essential Travel Tips for First-Timers

Embarking on your first trip to Alaska can be an extraordinary adventure, but careful preparation is essential for maximizing your experience. Here are some helpful tips to consider while planning:

1. **Plan Ahead**: The prime travel season in Alaska runs from June to August. To ensure availability and secure better rates, book your accommodations, tours, and transportation at least six months in advance.
2. **Dress in Layers**: The weather can shift rapidly, even in summer. Bring waterproof jackets, insulated clothing, and sturdy footwear. Anticipate summer temperatures ranging from 50°F to 70°F (10°C to 21°C) and significantly colder conditions in winter.
3. **Transportation**: Renting a car is an excellent way to explore regions like the Kenai Peninsula or Denali. Rental prices typically start at $50 to $100

per day. If you plan to visit coastal areas, consider using the Alaska Marine Highway ferries, which cost between $50 and $150 per person.

4. **Wildlife Safety**: Always keep a safe distance from wildlife—300 feet (91 meters) from bears and 100 yards (91 meters) from marine mammals. When hiking, carry bear spray, which usually costs around $40 to $50.

5. **Honor Local Customs**: Alaska is home to numerous Indigenous communities. Consider visiting cultural institutions, such as the Alaska Native Heritage Center in Anchorage (admission: $29.95 for adults), to gain insights into their traditions.

6. **Prepare for Limited Connectivity**: Cell service can be unreliable in remote areas. It's wise to download offline maps and carry a physical map as a backup.

Chapter 2: Anchorage

When to Visit

The best time to visit Anchorage depends on the activities and experiences you're looking for, as each season offers something unique.

Summer (June to August) is the most popular time to visit, with long daylight hours and temperatures ranging from 55°F to 70°F (13°C to 21°C). This is the ideal season for outdoor activities like hiking Flattop Mountain, biking the Tony Knowles Coastal Trail, or fishing for salmon in Ship Creek. Events like the Anchorage Market and the Girdwood Forest Fair (30 miles/48 km south) add to the lively atmosphere. Hotel rates during summer range from $150 - $300 per night, so book early.

Fall (September to October) brings cooler temperatures (40°F–55°F or 4°C–13°C) and stunning fall foliage. It's a quieter time to visit, with fewer crowds and lower accommodation prices. This is also a great time for Northern Lights viewing, especially in late September.

Winter (November to March) transforms Anchorage into a snowy wonderland. Temperatures can drop to 5°F (-15°C), so pack warm layers. Popular activities include skiing at Alyeska Resort (40 miles/64 km away), dog sledding, and attending the Fur Rendezvous Festival in February.

Spring (April to May) offers milder weather (30°F–50°F or -1°C–10°C) and the chance to see wildlife emerging from hibernation. The Anchorage Museum and Alaska Native Heritage Center are great year-round attractions.

Choose your visit based on the season that aligns with your interests, and Anchorage will not disappoint.

Top Attractions in Anchorage

Top Attractions in Anchorage

As Alaska's largest city, Anchorage boasts a blend of cultural sites, outdoor activities, and unique attractions. Here are seven must-see locations:

1. **Alaska Native Heritage Center**: Discover the rich Indigenous cultures of Alaska through interactive exhibits, traditional homes, and live performances.

Admission is $29.95 for adults and $19.95 for children. Located just 10 miles (16 km) from downtown, it's easily accessible by car or shuttle.

2. **Anchorage Museum at Rasmuson Center**: This premier museum showcases exhibitions focused on Alaskan history, art, and science. Admission costs $20 for adults and $10 for children, and it is conveniently situated in downtown Anchorage.

3. **Tony Knowles Coastal Trail**: Stretching 11 miles (18 km), this picturesque trail is ideal for biking or walking, providing breathtaking views of Cook Inlet and the Chugach Mountains. Bike rentals start at $20 per hour.

4. **Flattop Mountain**: A favorite hiking destination located only 13 miles (21 km) from downtown, Flattop offers sweeping vistas of Anchorage and the surrounding area. Parking at the trailhead is available for $5.

5. **Kincaid Park**: Situated 10 miles (16 km) from downtown, this expansive park is perfect for wildlife watching, hiking, and cross-country skiing. Entrance is free.

6. **Alaska Aviation Museum**: Delve into Alaska's aviation history with a collection of vintage aircraft and engaging exhibits. Admission costs $17 for adults and $8 for children. The museum is located near Lake Hood, about 4 miles (6.4 km) from downtown.

7. **Earthquake Park**: This park honors the 1964 Good Friday Earthquake and features interpretive signs and trails. Admission is free, and it's located just 4 miles (6.4 km) from downtown.

Outdoor Activities and Day Trips

Anchorage serves as an excellent launching point for discovering Alaska's stunning natural landscapes, providing a range of outdoor activities and day trips to suit various interests.

Hiking

For those who love hiking, the Flattop Mountain Trail is a must-visit. Situated just 13 miles (21 km) from downtown Anchorage, this 3.3-mile (5.3-km) round-trip hike rewards adventurers with sweeping views of the city and the surrounding mountains. Parking at the trailhead is available for $5. If you prefer a more leisurely experience, the Tony Knowles Coastal Trail is an 11-mile (18-km) paved route perfect for walking or biking, with bike rentals starting at $20 per hour.

Wildlife Tours

Wildlife enthusiasts can embark on a guided tour to the Alaska Wildlife Conservation Center, located 47 miles (75 km) south of Anchorage. Admission is $17 for adults, and visitors can observe rescued bears, moose, and bison in a natural habitat. For those interested in marine wildlife, consider taking a day cruise from Whittier (60 miles/96 km away) into Prince William Sound, where you might encounter whales, sea otters, and puffins. Cruise prices start at $150 per person.

Scenic Drives

The Seward Highway, recognized as a National Scenic Byway, provides breathtaking views of Turnagain Arm and the Chugach Mountains. Make a stop at Beluga Point (20 miles/32 km from Anchorage) to search for beluga whales, or continue on to Portage Glacier (50 miles/80 km) for a short hike and stunning glacier vistas.

Where to Stay and Eat

Anchorage provides a diverse range of accommodations and dining options to cater to all budgets and tastes.

Where to Stay

For a luxurious experience, consider the Hotel Captain Cook in downtown Anchorage, which features top-notch amenities and breathtaking views of Cook Inlet. Room rates begin at $300 per night. If you're looking for a mid-range option, the Alyeska Resort in Girdwood (40 miles/64 km from Anchorage) offers a serene mountain retreat, with rates starting at $200. Budget-conscious travelers may prefer the Bent Prop Inn & Hostel in Midtown, where dormitory beds start at $40 per night.

Where to Eat

For an upscale dining experience, visit Crow's Nest (located downtown), which specializes in exquisite seafood and steaks while offering panoramic views; dinner prices range from $50 to $100 per person. For a more casual atmosphere, Moose's Tooth Pub & Pizzeria is a local favorite, known for its inventive pizzas and craft beers, with meals costing between $15 and $30. If you're after breakfast, don't miss Snow City Café, famous for its crab omelets and reindeer sausage, with meal prices averaging between $15 and $25.

Chapter 3: Fairbanks

Exploring Fairbanks' History and Culture

Fairbanks, often referred to as the "Golden Heart City," is steeped in history and culture, providing visitors with insights into Alaska's heritage and lively traditions. Begin your exploration at the University of Alaska Museum of the North, situated 4 miles (6.4 km) from downtown. Admission is $16 for adults and $9 for children, and the museum showcases exhibits on Indigenous cultures, the gold rush era, and local wildlife, alongside an impressive collection of Native art.

Next, make your way to the Morris Thompson Cultural and Visitors Center, a complimentary attraction in downtown Fairbanks. This center highlights exhibits on Native traditions, seasonal activities, and the history of the Interior region.

For an interactive experience, visit Pioneer Park, located just 2 miles (3.2 km) from downtown. This expansive 44-

acre park features historic structures, a replica of a gold rush town, and the SS Nenana, a historic sternwheeler. While entry is free, some attractions within the park may charge nominal fees.

Be sure to check out the Fountainhead Antique Auto Museum, which is 3 miles (4.8 km) from downtown. Admission is $12, and this museum merges vintage automobiles with displays focused on Fairbanks' early 20th-century history.

Northern Lights Viewing

Fairbanks is renowned as one of the premier locations in the world for witnessing the Northern Lights, thanks to its position directly beneath the auroral oval.

Best Times to Visit

The Northern Lights are most prominently visible from late August to mid-April when the nights are dark and clear. The optimal viewing hours are typically between 10 PM and 3 AM. Spending at least three nights in Fairbanks significantly boosts your chances of seeing the aurora, with a success rate of 80–90% during this timeframe.

Top Viewing Locations

- **Aurora Pointe**: Located just 20 minutes (16 km) from downtown Fairbanks, this facility features a comfortable indoor area where visitors can enjoy snacks and hot beverages for $50 per person.

- **Chena Hot Springs Resort**: Situated about 60 miles (97 km) from Fairbanks, this destination offers the unique experience of viewing the aurora while soaking in natural hot springs. Day passes begin at $15.

- **Murphy Dome**: A short 25-mile (40 km) drive from Fairbanks, this elevated site provides unobstructed views of the night sky.

Photography Tips

- Use a tripod to stabilize your camera.

- Set your camera to manual mode with a high ISO (800–3200), a wide aperture (f/2.8 or lower), and a long exposure time (10–20 seconds).

- Bring extra batteries, as cold temperatures can quickly deplete them.

Hot Springs, Wildlife, and Unique Experiences

Fairbanks presents a range of unique experiences that showcase its stunning natural scenery and rich cultural heritage. A visit to Chena Hot Springs Resort, located 60 miles (97 km) northeast of Fairbanks, is essential. Here, you can relax in the natural hot springs surrounded by snowy landscapes in the winter or vibrant greenery in the summer. Day passes begin at $15, and the resort also features an Ice Museum, home to exquisite ice sculptures.

For wildlife lovers, the Running Reindeer Ranch, just 10 miles (16 km) from downtown, offers a memorable adventure. Participate in a guided nature walk alongside a herd of friendly reindeer for $75 per person and gain insights into these fascinating creatures in their natural environment.

Fairbanks also hosts various seasonal festivals that celebrate its distinctive culture. The World Ice Art Championships in March feature breathtaking ice sculptures, while the Midnight Sun Festival in June honors the summer solstice with live music, food, and local crafts.

Chapter 4: Glaciers, Fjords, and Coastal Wonders

Cruising the Inside Passage

Exploring Alaska's Inside Passage by cruise is one of the most breathtaking and unforgettable ways to take in the state's natural wonders. This route spans over 500 miles (805 km), starting from Puget Sound in Washington, winding through British Columbia, and extending into Alaska's southeastern panhandle. It consists of a series of waterways framed by majestic mountains, lush forests, and stunning glacial landscapes.

Well-known cruise lines such as Holland America, Princess Cruises, and Royal Caribbean offer itineraries that range from 7 to 14 days, with prices beginning at around $100 per person per night for interior cabins. For a more personalized experience, small-ship operators like UnCruise Adventures and Alaskan Dream Cruises provide access to secluded coves and lesser-known ports.

Highlights along the Inside Passage include Glacier Bay National Park, where visitors can observe colossal glaciers calving into the ocean, and Tracy Arm Fjord, famous for its striking cliffs and waterfalls. Stops at historic towns such as Juneau, Ketchikan, and Skagway provide chances to delve into Alaska's Gold Rush history, explore Native cultural sites, and partake in outdoor activities like dog sledding and whale watching.

Wildlife abounds along this route, offering opportunities to see humpback whales, orcas, sea lions, and bald eagles. Many cruises feature naturalist presentations and ranger-led programs to deepen your understanding of the region's ecology.

Highlights of Juneau, Ketchikan, Petersburg, Wrangell, and Sitka

Alaska's coastal towns along the Inside Passage are steeped in history, culture, and stunning natural beauty. Each town presents unique experiences, from exploring Indigenous heritage to witnessing remarkable wildlife and landscapes.

Juneau

As the capital of Alaska, Juneau is a center for history, culture, and outdoor adventure. One of its standout attractions is the Mendenhall Glacier, located just 12 miles (19 km) from downtown. Visitors can hike trails such as the Nugget Falls Trail or join guided kayaking tours for close-up views. Shuttle service to the glacier is available for around $45 round trip, which includes a $5 fee for the visitor center.

For a panoramic view of the city, take a ride on the Goldbelt Mount Roberts Tramway, ascending 1,800 feet (549 meters) to scenic trails and a cultural center. Tickets are priced at $45 for adults. The Alaska State Museum in downtown Juneau offers exhibits on Indigenous cultures, Russian colonization, and the Gold Rush, providing an in-depth look at the region's history, with admission costing $14 for adults.

Juneau is also an excellent location for whale watching. Tours in Auke Bay, about 15 miles (24 km) from downtown, range from $120 to $150 per person and frequently include sightings of humpback whales, orcas, and sea lions.

Ketchikan

Known as the "Salmon Capital of the World," Ketchikan is celebrated for its fishing culture and Native heritage. Begin your visit at Totem Bight State Historical Park, situated 10 miles (16 km) from downtown. The park features 14 restored totem poles and a replica clan house. Admission is free, and guided tours are offered for a small fee.

Another highlight is Creek Street, a historic boardwalk built on stilts over Ketchikan Creek. Once a red-light district, it now houses shops, galleries, and Dolly's House Museum, which provides insights into the town's colorful past. Admission to the museum is $10.

Outdoor enthusiasts should not miss a day trip to Misty Fjords National Monument. Accessible by boat or floatplane, this pristine wilderness showcases dramatic cliffs, waterfalls, and abundant wildlife. Tours start at $250 per person.

Petersburg

Often referred to as "Little Norway," Petersburg is a quaint fishing town with a rich Norwegian heritage. The Sons of Norway Hall serves as the town's cultural center, where visitors can learn about local traditions and attend events like the annual Little Norway Festival in May.

Petersburg also serves as a gateway to LeConte Glacier, the southernmost tidewater glacier in North America. Small boat tours to the glacier start at $200 per person and often include opportunities to spot seals and calving icebergs.

Frederick Sound is an excellent location for whale watching, with humpback whales frequently feeding in these waters during the summer. Tours typically cost between $150 and $200 per person.

Wrangell

Wrangell is a quieter destination, ideal for travelers seeking off-the-beaten-path adventures. A top attraction is the Anan Creek Wildlife Observatory, located 30 miles (48 km) from town. Accessible by boat, this site offers a rare opportunity to see black and brown bears fishing for salmon. Guided tours start at $300 per person.

History enthusiasts will appreciate Petroglyph Beach State Historic Site, just 1 mile (1.6 km) from downtown, where ancient rock carvings reveal the area's Indigenous history. Admission is free, with interpretive signs providing context for the petroglyphs.

Another cultural highlight is the Chief Shakes Tribal House, situated on Shakes Island in Wrangell Harbor. This reconstructed Tlingit clan house offers guided tours for $10 per person.

Sitka

Sitka, once the capital of Russian America, blends Indigenous and Russian history. Start your visit at Sitka National Historical Park, where trails lined with totem poles lead to the site of the 1804 Battle of Sitka. The visitor center features exhibits on Tlingit culture and Russian colonization, and admission is free.

The Russian Bishop's House is a well-preserved example of Russian colonial architecture, with guided tours available for $8 per person. Nearby, St. Michael's Cathedral, a replica of the original 1848 Russian Orthodox church, is another essential site to visit.

For wildlife enthusiasts, the Fortress of the Bear is a rescue center for orphaned bears located 5 miles (8 km) from downtown, with admission costing $15 for adults. Sitka is also a great spot for marine wildlife tours, offering chances to see sea otters, whales, and puffins, with tours starting at $150 per person.

Practical Tips for Visiting

- **Transportation**: Most towns are accessible via the Alaska Marine Highway ferries or small regional flights, with ferry fares ranging from $50 to $150 per person, depending on the route.

- **Weather**: The Inside Passage has a temperate rainforest climate, so be sure to pack waterproof clothing and sturdy shoes.

- **Local Cuisine**: Don't miss the opportunity to try fresh seafood, including salmon, halibut, and king crab, at local restaurants in each town. Meals typically range from $15 to $30 per person.

Whale Watching and Glacier Adventures

The Inside Passage is one of Alaska's prime destinations for whale watching and glacier exploration, offering visitors unforgettable experiences with marine wildlife and stunning icy vistas.

Whale Watching

Humpback whales, orcas, and gray whales are frequently seen in the Inside Passage, especially during the summer months (May to September). Key whale-watching locations include Juneau, Sitka, and Petersburg.

- **Juneau**: Auke Bay is an excellent spot for whale-watching tours. Companies like Harv and Marv's Outback Alaska and Juneau Whale Watch provide small-group tours starting at $120 to $150 per person. These excursions often feature humpback whales engaging in bubble-net feeding, as well as sea lions and bald eagles.

- **Sitka**: Sitka Sound is renowned for its rich marine life, including orcas and sea otters. Tours offered by operators like Allen Marine Tours start at $150 per person and include knowledgeable naturalist guides.

- **Petersburg**: Frederick Sound is a prime area for observing humpback whales. Small boat tours from Alaska Sea Adventures offer close encounters with wildlife for approximately $200 per person.

Glacier Adventures

The Inside Passage boasts some of Alaska's most breathtaking glaciers, many of which can be accessed by boat, kayak, or small plane.

- **Mendenhall Glacier (Juneau)**: Located 12 miles (19 km) from downtown, this glacier can be reached via shuttle bus for around $45 round trip. Visitors can hike trails such as the Nugget Falls Trail or participate in guided kayaking tours starting at $150 per person.

- **Tracy Arm Fjord (near Juneau)**: This fjord features impressive cliffs, waterfalls, and the twin Sawyer Glaciers. Boat tours to Tracy Arm begin at $200 per person and often include wildlife sightings.

- **LeConte Glacier (Petersburg)**: As the southernmost tidewater glacier in North America, LeConte Glacier is accessible through small boat tours that start at $200 per person. These tours typically offer views of calving icebergs and seals lounging on ice floes.

Tips for Travelers

- **Book Early**: Tours tend to fill up fast during peak season, so it's wise to secure your reservations in advance.

- **Dress Warmly**: Even in summer, temperatures on the water can be brisk. Wear layers, waterproof clothing, and sturdy footwear.

- **Bring Binoculars and Cameras**: Binoculars will enhance your wildlife viewing experience, while a camera with a zoom lens is perfect for capturing stunning images of glaciers and whales.

Chapter 5: Denali National Park and Beyond

Trails, Wildlife, and Scenic Drives

Denali National Park, encompassing over 6 million acres, stands as one of Alaska's most renowned destinations. Famous for its towering peaks, including Denali (20,310 feet), the highest mountain in North America, the park offers a blend of hiking trails, wildlife viewing, and scenic drives that highlight its stunning wilderness. Whether you're an enthusiastic hiker, a wildlife lover, or simply looking for a scenic road trip, Denali has something for everyone.

Top Trails in Denali

While Denali is celebrated for its extensive wilderness and off-trail hiking options, several maintained trails near the park entrance cater to various skill levels:

1. **Horseshoe Lake Trail**

- **Distance**: 2 miles (3.2 km) round trip
- **Difficulty**: Easy
- This family-friendly trail leads to a tranquil lake surrounded by forest, making it a great spot for birdwatching and occasional beaver sightings.

2. **Mount Healy Overlook Trail**
   - **Distance**: 4.9 miles (7.9 km) round trip
   - **Difficulty**: Moderate to strenuous
   - This trail offers a challenging ascent with rewarding panoramic views of the park and surrounding valleys. Plan for a 3–4 hour hike.

3. **Savage River Loop Trail**
   - **Distance**: 2 miles (3.2 km) round trip
   - **Difficulty**: Easy to moderate
   - Located 15 miles (24 km) into the park, this trail follows the Savage River and provides chances to spot Dall sheep on nearby cliffs.

4. **Triple Lakes Trail**

    - **Distance**: 9.5 miles (15.3 km) one way
    - **Difficulty**: Moderate
    - This longer trail meanders through forests and past three picturesque lakes, perfect for those seeking a quieter hike.

For seasoned hikers, Denali's backcountry offers countless opportunities for exploration. Overnight trips require permits, and visitors should be prepared for rugged terrain and unpredictable weather.

Wildlife Viewing Opportunities

Denali is home to Alaska's "Big Five": grizzly bears, moose, caribou, wolves, and Dall sheep. Wildlife sightings are common along the park road, especially in open tundra areas.

- **Best Times for Wildlife Viewing**: Early mornings and late evenings are optimal for spotting animals. Summer (June to August) is the peak season for wildlife activity.

- **Popular Locations**: Polychrome Pass (Mile 46) and Eielson Visitor Center (Mile 66) are known for frequent wildlife sightings. The braided rivers near Toklat River (Mile 53) are also hotspots for caribou and bears.

- **Tips**: Always maintain a safe distance—at least 300 feet (91 meters) from bears and 25 yards (23 meters) from other wildlife. Binoculars or a zoom lens enhance the viewing experience.

Scenic Drives in Denali

The Denali Park Road, the only road in the park, stretches 92 miles (148 km) from the entrance to Kantishna. Private vehicles can travel the first 15 miles (24 km); beyond that, visitors must use park buses.

1. **Savage River (Mile 15)**

    o This is the furthest point accessible by private vehicle, offering breathtaking views of the Alaska Range and opportunities to see wildlife.

2. **Polychrome Pass (Mile 46)**
   - Renowned for its colorful volcanic rock formations, this section of the road presents some of the park's most dramatic vistas.

3. **Eielson Visitor Center (Mile 66)**
   - This stop offers sweeping views of Denali (weather permitting) and access to short hiking trails. The visitor center features exhibits about the park's geology and wildlife.

4. **Wonder Lake (Mile 85)**
   - A highlight of the park road, Wonder Lake is a stunning glacial lake that reflects Denali on clear days, making it a prime spot for photography and birdwatching.

Park Bus Options

To explore beyond Mile 15, visitors can choose from various bus options:

- **Transit Buses**: These hop-on, hop-off buses provide flexibility for hiking and wildlife viewing. Tickets start at $30 per person.

- **Tour Buses**: Guided tours with narration are available, such as the Tundra Wilderness Tour ($140 per person) or the Kantishna Experience ($240 per person). These tours include stops at key viewpoints and wildlife spotting opportunities.

Tips for Visiting Denali

- **Weather**: Denali's weather can be unpredictable, with summer temperatures ranging from 30°F to 70°F (-1°C to 21°C). Dress in layers and bring rain gear.

- **Reservations**: Bus tickets and campgrounds fill up quickly during the peak season (June to August). It's advisable to book in advance to secure your spot.

- **Safety**: Carry bear spray while hiking and follow Leave No Trace principles to help protect the park's natural environment.

Camping and Lodging Options

Denali National Park provides a variety of camping and lodging options to accommodate all types of travelers, from basic tent sites to comfortable lodges. Whether you want to fully immerse yourself in nature or prefer modern conveniences, this guide will help you plan your stay.

Camping in Denali

Denali features six campgrounds, five of which are accessible via the Denali Park Road. Reservations are strongly advised, especially during the busy summer months (June to August).

1. **Riley Creek Campground (Mile 0.25)**
    - Open year-round, this campground is close to the park entrance and offers 147 sites for tents and RVs. Amenities include flush toilets, potable water, and a dump station. Rates start at $20 per night.

2. **Savage River Campground (Mile 13)**

    o Situated 13 miles (21 km) into the park, this campground has 33 sites for tents and RVs. It serves as an excellent base for hiking the Savage River Loop Trail. Sites cost $20 per night.

3. **Teklanika River Campground (Mile 29)**

    o Perfect for those wanting to venture further into the park, this campground offers 53 sites for tents and RVs, but requires a minimum three-night stay. Sites are priced at $20 per night, and campers must use the park's transit buses for access beyond this point.

4. **Wonder Lake Campground (Mile 85)**

    o This tent-only campground near Wonder Lake provides breathtaking views of Denali on clear days. It is remote and requires a lengthy bus ride for access. Sites cost $20 per night.

Tips for Campers:

- **Book Early**: Reserve your spot through the National Park Service website, as campgrounds tend to fill quickly.

- **Food Storage**: Use bear-proof containers or the provided food lockers to safely store your food.

- **Dress Warmly**: Bring warm clothing, as nighttime temperatures can drop significantly, even in summer.

Lodging in and Around Denali

For those seeking more comfort, several lodges and accommodations are available near the park entrance and within the park itself.

1. **Denali Bluffs Hotel**

    o Located just outside the park entrance, this hotel features cozy rooms with mountain views. Rates start at $250 per night during peak season.

2. **McKinley Chalet Resort**

    o Situated along the Nenana River, this resort offers modern rooms, dining options, and shuttle services to the park. Rates begin at $300 per night.

3. **Kantishna Roadhouse (Mile 92)**

    o Nestled deep within the park, this all-inclusive lodge provides rustic cabins, meals, and guided activities. Rates start at $600 per person per night, including transportation.

4. **Denali Backcountry Lodge (Mile 92)**

    o Another remote option, this lodge offers private cabins, meals, and guided hikes. Rates begin at $700 per person per night.

Tips for Lodging:

- **Reserve Early**: Book accommodations well in advance, as availability is limited during the summer.

- **Consider Healy**: Look into staying in Healy, 11 miles (18 km) north of the park entrance, for more budget-friendly motels and cabins.

Safety Tips

- **Wildlife**: Always secure your food to avoid attracting bears, and maintain a safe distance from wildlife.

- **Weather**: Be ready for sudden weather changes. Pack rain gear and warm layers.

- **Reservations**: Make reservations for both camping and lodging as early as possible to ensure your preferred dates.

Off-the-Beaten-Path Adventures

The Denali region offers much more than its iconic mountain and popular trails. For those in search of unique and tranquil experiences, there are numerous hidden gems and lesser-known activities that highlight the area's rugged beauty and solitude. Here are some off-the-beaten-path adventures to explore:

1. Savage River Waterfall

While the Savage River Loop Trail (2 miles/3.2 km) is well-known, few visitors continue past the "End of

Maintained Trail" sign. By following the unmarked path along the river, you'll uncover a breathtaking waterfall cascading over rocks. This moderate hike involves some scrambling, so be sure to wear sturdy footwear. The trailhead is located 15 miles (24 km) into Denali National Park and is accessible by car or the free Savage River Shuttle.

2. 8-Mile Lake

Situated off Stampede Road, 8-Mile Lake is a hidden treasure just outside the park. This serene spot is ideal for a peaceful picnic, berry picking in late summer, or even viewing the Northern Lights in the fall. The lake is 8 miles (13 km) from the George Parks Highway and can be reached by car, making it a great alternative to the busier Wonder Lake.

3. Dragonfly Creek Waterfall

For a distinct hiking experience that begins with a descent, visit Dragonfly Creek near Mile 242 of the George Parks Highway. Park at the pull-off and follow the trail into the woods. After a short walk, you'll arrive at the creek, which leads to a stunning waterfall. This hike requires some bushwhacking and creek crossings, so waterproof shoes are advisable.

4. Wilderness Off-Trail Hike

For a guided off-trail experience, consider the Wilderness Wonders Off-Trail Interpretive Hike. This 4-hour tour takes you into the boreal forest just outside the park, where you'll learn about the ecosystem while navigating through mossy terrain. Tours start at $100 per person and include expert guidance.

5. Rafting the Nenana River

For those seeking an adrenaline rush, rafting on the Nenana River is a must-try. This adventure features a mix of calm waters and Class III-IV rapids, all set against the stunning backdrop of the Alaska Range. Half-day trips begin at $100 per person and are offered by local operators in the Denali area.

6. Fox Creek Gorge

Near Dragonfly Creek, Fox Creek Gorge presents a technical hike through a rocky chute leading to a 35-foot waterfall. This short but challenging hike is perfect for those looking for a quick adventure. The trailhead is marked along the George Parks Highway, and the hike takes about an hour round trip.

Tips for Off-the-Beaten-Path Adventures

- **Prioritize Safety**: Always inform someone of your plans and expected return time. Cell service is limited, so carry a map or GPS device.

- **Gear Up**: Wear sturdy hiking boots, dress in layers, and bring bear spray ($40 - $50).

- **Respect Nature**: Adhere to Leave No Trace principles to help preserve these pristine areas.

Chapter 6: The Arctic Circle and Remote Alaska

Crossing the Arctic Circle

Crossing the Arctic Circle is a dream adventure for many travelers, offering an opportunity to explore one of the most remote and pristine areas on the planet. Situated at 66°33' north latitude, the Arctic Circle marks the southernmost point where the sun remains visible for 24 hours during the summer solstice and disappears for the same duration during the winter solstice. Here's what you can anticipate when venturing into this remarkable part of Alaska.

Unique Landscapes

The Arctic Circle is characterized by its rugged and untouched wilderness. Visitors can expect expansive tundra plains, rolling hills, and striking mountain ranges. In summer, the landscape is vibrant with wildflowers and interlaced with rivers and streams. In winter, the region transforms into a snow-covered paradise, featuring frozen lakes and vast icy expanses.

One of the most notable phenomena in the Arctic is the Midnight Sun during summer, providing continuous daylight and creating a surreal atmosphere. In contrast, winter presents the opportunity to witness the Northern Lights, with dazzling displays of green, pink, and purple illuminating the night sky.

Experiences and Activities

- **Dalton Highway Adventure**: The Dalton Highway, commonly known as the "Haul Road," serves as the main route to the Arctic Circle. Beginning near Fairbanks, this highway stretches 414 miles (666 km) to Prudhoe Bay. The Arctic Circle is found at Mile 115, which is about a 6-hour drive from Fairbanks. Guided tours along the Dalton Highway start at $250 per person and often include stops at the Yukon River and Finger Mountain.

- **Arctic Circle Signpost**: At Mile 115, visitors can stop at the Arctic Circle signpost for a photo opportunity and receive an official Arctic Circle Certificate.

- **Wildlife Viewing**: The Arctic is home to fascinating wildlife, including caribou, musk oxen, Arctic foxes, and various migratory birds. Keep an eye out for these animals, especially in summer when they are most active.

- **Cultural Experiences**: Many tours offer visits to Indigenous communities, allowing travelers to learn about the traditions and lifestyles of Alaska's Native peoples.

Practical Tips for Travelers

- **Weather**: The Arctic is known for its extreme conditions. Summer temperatures typically range from 40°F to 60°F (4°C to 15°C), while winter temperatures can plummet to -40°F (-40°C). Dress in layers and bring waterproof gear.

- **Road Conditions**: The Dalton Highway is primarily gravel and can be challenging to navigate. If you choose to drive, ensure your vehicle is equipped with spare tires, extra fuel, and emergency supplies.

- **Guided Tours**: For those unfamiliar with the area, guided tours are highly recommended. They provide transportation, knowledgeable guides, and safety equipment, making the journey more manageable and enjoyable.

- **Timing**: Summer (June to August) is the optimal time for road travel and wildlife viewing, while winter (November to March) is best for those looking to see the Northern Lights.

Barrow (Utqiaġvik) and Nome

Barrow (Utqiaġvik) and Nome are two of Alaska's most remote and intriguing communities, providing visitors with an insight into life in the Far North. Both towns are rich in history, shaped by their unique Arctic surroundings, and deeply infused with Indigenous culture. Here's why these destinations are worth your exploration.

Barrow (Utqiaġvik)

Situated 320 miles (515 km) north of the Arctic Circle, Utqiaġvik (previously known as Barrow) is the northernmost community in the United States, home to around 4,300 residents, primarily Iñupiat, Alaska Natives with a profound connection to the land and sea.

Culture and History

The history of Utqiaġvik stretches back over 1,500 years, with archaeological evidence of early Iñupiat settlements. A visit to the Iñupiat Heritage Center is essential, featuring exhibits on traditional whaling, subsistence living, and the Iñupiat way of life. Admission is $10 for adults and $5 for children. The Nalukataq Whaling Festival in June is a highlight, celebrating the successful whaling season with traditional dances, food, and the famous blanket toss.

Attractions

A prominent landmark is the Whale Bone Arch, constructed from the jawbones of a bowhead whale, located on the edge of the Arctic Ocean—perfect for memorable photos. Nearby, the Cape Smythe Whaling and Trading Station, built in 1893, is the oldest frame structure in the Arctic and a designated National Historic Landmark.

Unique Experiences

Utqiaġvik offers rare opportunities to view polar bears, snowy owls, and other Arctic wildlife. Guided tours to Point Barrow, the northernmost point in the U.S., cost around $100 per person. In winter, visitors can marvel at the Northern Lights, while summer brings the Midnight Sun, offering 24 hours of daylight from May to August.

Nome

Located on the southern Seward Peninsula, Nome is a historic gold rush town with a population of approximately 3,800. It is accessible by air and is celebrated for its rugged landscapes, rich history, and vibrant culture.

Culture and History

Nome's history is closely linked to the 1898 gold rush, which attracted thousands of prospectors to the area. The town honors its gold rush heritage with events like Nome Gold Rush Days in September. The Carrie M. McLain Memorial Museum offers insights into Nome's history, featuring artifacts from the gold rush and the region's Indigenous peoples. Admission is $5 for adults.

Attractions

Nome is renowned as the finish line for the Iditarod Trail Sled Dog Race, held each March. Visitors can explore the town's gold dredges and embark on a self-guided tour of the abandoned mining camps along the Nome-Council

Road, which also offers stunning views of the Bering Sea and opportunities to spot musk oxen and reindeer.

Unique Experiences

Nome's beaches are popular for gold panning, an enjoyable activity for visitors, with equipment rentals starting at $20 per day. The town is also a birdwatching hotspot, with species such as the Arctic Warbler and Yellow Wagtail commonly seen. In winter, Nome provides dog sledding tours and a chance to experience the stark beauty of the icy tundra.

Practical Tips for Visiting

- **Getting There**: Utqiaġvik and Nome are accessible only by air, with Alaska Airlines offering regular flights from Anchorage and Fairbanks, with round-trip fares starting at $500.

- **Weather**: Both towns experience extreme weather conditions. Summer temperatures range from 40°F to 60°F (4°C to 15°C), while winter temperatures can plummet to -40°F (-40°C). Dress in layers and pack waterproof gear.

- **Accommodations**: In Utqiaġvik, the Top of the World Hotel offers rooms starting at $275 per night. In Nome, options include the Aurora Inn, with rates beginning at $200 per night.

Indigenous Culture and Traditions

Alaska boasts a rich and diverse Indigenous heritage, encompassing over 20 distinct Native cultures and more than 200 federally recognized tribes. These communities have coexisted with the land for millennia, maintaining traditions, art, and languages that continue to flourish today. For travelers, engaging with Alaska's Indigenous cultures provides a unique chance to connect with the state's history and its people while supporting local communities.

Cultural Centers and Museums

Begin your exploration at the Alaska Native Heritage Center in Anchorage, a central hub for learning about the state's Indigenous groups. The center features traditional dwellings, live performances of drumming and dancing, and storytelling sessions. Admission is $29.95 for adults and $19.95 for children. Located just 10 miles (16 km) from downtown Anchorage, it is easily reachable by car or shuttle.

In Fairbanks, the Morris Thompson Cultural and Visitors Center offers free admission and presents exhibits on Athabascan traditions, subsistence lifestyles, and seasonal activities. Nearby, the University of Alaska Museum of the North showcases an extensive collection of Native art and artifacts, with admission priced at $16 for adults.

Traditional Art and Crafts

Alaska Native art reflects a profound connection to the environment. Totem poles, crafted by the Tlingit, Haida, and Tsimshian peoples of Southeast Alaska, narrate stories of ancestry and culture. Visit the Totem Heritage Center in Ketchikan or Sitka National Historical Park to see these impressive works. Admission to the Totem Heritage Center is $6 for adults.

In Southwest Alaska, the Yup'ik and Cup'ik peoples are renowned for their intricate masks and woven baskets, while the Iñupiat of the Arctic create beautiful ivory carvings and baleen baskets. Many cultural centers and local galleries offer authentic Native art—look for the

"Silver Hand" emblem to ensure your purchase supports Indigenous artists.

Respectful Engagement

When visiting Indigenous communities or participating in cultural activities, it is essential to show respect. Always ask for permission before taking photographs, particularly during ceremonies or in private spaces. Learning a few words in the local language, such as "quyana" (thank you in Yup'ik), can demonstrate appreciation.

Travelers can also participate in festivals like Celebration in Juneau, held every two years, which features traditional singing, dancing, and regalia. Tickets typically range from $30 to $50 for a day pass.

Chapter 7: Wildlife Encounters and Nature Exploration

Alaska's Big Five

Alaska's Big Five—moose, bears, wolves, caribou, and Dall sheep—showcase the state's remarkable wildlife diversity and are a major draw for many visitors. Spotting these iconic animals in their natural habitats can be a memorable experience, but it requires careful planning, patience, and respect for the environment.

1. Moose

Moose are the largest members of the deer family and are commonly found in Alaska's forests, wetlands, and along riverbanks. Weighing up to 1,500 pounds, they are often seen grazing on willows and aquatic plants.
Where to Spot Them:

- **Denali National Park:** Moose are frequently seen near the park entrance and along the Savage River.

- **Anchorage:** Kincaid Park and the Tony Knowles Coastal Trail are great locations for viewing moose, especially during early morning or late evening. **Viewing Tips:** Maintain a safe distance of at least 75 feet (23 meters). Moose can become aggressive, particularly during mating season in the fall and when protecting calves in the spring.

2. Bears

Alaska is home to three species of bears: grizzly (brown), black, and polar bears. Grizzlies are often spotted in coastal regions and national parks, while black bears are more prevalent in forested areas. Polar bears inhabit the Arctic.
Where to Spot Them:

- **Katmai National Park:** Known for bear viewing at Brooks Falls, where grizzlies catch salmon mid-air. Tours start at around $950 per person, including a floatplane ride from King Salmon.

- **Admiralty Island:** Often referred to as the "Fortress of the Bears," this island near Juneau has one of the highest concentrations of brown bears globally.
  Viewing Tips: Always carry bear spray ($40 - $50)

when hiking. Stay at least 300 feet (91 meters) away, and never approach or feed bears. Joining guided tours is recommended for safe viewing.

3. Wolves

Wolves are elusive creatures, often heard before they are seen. These intelligent predators travel in packs across Alaska's wilderness, hunting caribou, moose, and smaller mammals.

Where to Spot Them:

- **Denali National Park:** Wolves can occasionally be spotted along the Denali Park Road, particularly near Polychrome Pass and the Toklat River.

- **Yukon-Charley Rivers National Preserve:** This remote area offers a chance to see wolves in their natural habitat, although sightings are rare. **Viewing Tips:** Use binoculars or a zoom lens to observe wolves from a distance. Avoid making loud noises or sudden movements that might disturb them.

4. Caribou

Caribou, also known as reindeer, are migratory animals that travel in large herds across Alaska's tundra. They are an essential part of Indigenous culture and subsistence lifestyles.

Where to Spot Them:

- **Denali National Park:** Caribou are often seen grazing in open tundra areas along the park road.
- **Arctic National Wildlife Refuge:** This remote region is home to the Porcupine Caribou Herd, one of the largest in North America. **Viewing Tips:** Maintain a distance of at least 100 yards (91 meters) to avoid disturbing the herd. Use a telephoto lens for close-up photography.

5. Dall Sheep

Dall sheep are recognized for their striking white coats and curved horns. They inhabit steep, rocky slopes, making them easier to spot with binoculars.

Where to Spot Them:

- **Denali National Park:** Look for Dall sheep on the cliffs near Polychrome Pass and the Savage River.

- **Chugach State Park:** The Turnagain Arm area, just south of Anchorage, is an excellent place for sightings.

  Viewing Tips: Bring binoculars or a spotting scope to observe Dall sheep from a safe distance. Avoid entering their habitat, as it can disturb them and damage the fragile environment.

General Wildlife Viewing Tips

- **Timing:** Early morning and late evening are the best times for wildlife viewing, as animals are most active during these hours.

- **Gear:** Bring binoculars ($50 - $200) and a camera with a zoom lens for enhanced viewing and photography.

- **Safety:** Always follow park regulations and maintain a safe distance from all wildlife. Never feed animals, as it can harm them and create dangerous situations.

- **Guided Tours:** Consider joining a guided wildlife tour for expert insights and a higher chance of sightings. Prices typically range from $100 to $300 per person, depending on the location and duration.

Birdwatching and Marine Life

Alaska is a paradise for birdwatchers and marine life enthusiasts, offering unmatched opportunities to observe a variety of species in their natural environments. From coastal waters brimming with marine mammals to bird sanctuaries inhabited by rare and migratory species, Alaska's wildlife is a highlight for any nature lover.

Birdwatching in Alaska

With over 500 bird species, Alaska is an exceptional destination for birdwatching.
Top Locations:

- **Potter Marsh (Anchorage):** Situated 10 miles (16 km) south of downtown Anchorage, this wetland is a prime spot for waterfowl, including trumpeter swans, northern pintails, and sandhill cranes. Entry is free, and boardwalks facilitate easy viewing.

- **St. Paul Island (Pribilof Islands):** Renowned for its puffins, auklets, and red-legged kittiwakes, this remote island is a must-visit for avid birdwatchers.

Guided tours begin at $2,500, including flights from Anchorage.

- **Kachemak Bay (Homer):** This area is perfect for spotting bald eagles, shorebirds, and a variety of seabirds. The annual Kachemak Bay Shorebird Festival in May celebrates the migration of over 100,000 birds.
Notable Species: Look out for bald eagles, puffins, Arctic terns, and golden plovers. Bringing binoculars ($50 - $200) and a bird identification guidebook is recommended.

Marine Life in Alaska

The coastal waters of Alaska are teeming with marine life, providing chances to see whales, sea otters, seals, and more.

Best Locations:

- **Kenai Fjords National Park (Seward):** Day cruises ($150 - $200 per person) offer close encounters with humpback whales, orcas, and sea lions.

- **Glacier Bay National Park:** Accessible by boat tours or cruises, this area is known for its humpback whales, harbor seals, and porpoises.

- **Prince William Sound (Whittier):** Kayaking tours ($100 - $150 per person) allow you to paddle alongside sea otters and observe puffins nesting on rocky cliffs.

- **Species to Look For:** Common sightings include humpback whales, orcas, sea otters, harbor seals, and Steller sea lions.

Tips for Wildlife Viewing

- **Timing:** Summer (May to September) is the ideal time for birdwatching and marine life viewing, as migratory birds and whales are most active during this period.

- **Gear:** Bring a camera with a zoom lens and dress in layers to stay comfortable in Alaska's unpredictable weather.

- **Guided Tours:** Consider joining guided birding or marine tours for expert insights and increased chances of sightings.

Responsible Wildlife Viewing Tips

Alaska's remarkable wildlife is one of its greatest attractions, but observing animals in their natural habitats requires care and respect to ensure both your safety and the well-being of the wildlife.

1. Maintain a Safe Distance

Always keep a safe distance from wildlife to prevent causing stress or danger. The National Park Service recommends the following distances:

- **300 feet (91 meters)** from bears and wolves.

- **100 yards (91 meters)** from marine mammals like whales and seals.

- **25 yards (23 meters)** from other animals, such as moose or caribou. Utilize binoculars or a zoom lens to observe animals closely without disturbing them. Binoculars typically start at $50, while a quality zoom lens can range from $200 to $500.

2. Avoid Feeding Wildlife

Feeding animals disrupts their natural behaviors and can lead to dependency on humans, resulting in potentially dangerous encounters. Always store food securely in bear-proof containers while camping or hiking. Many parks offer bear-proof container rentals for $5 to $10 per day.

3. Stay Quiet and Respectful

Keep noise to a minimum to avoid startling wildlife. Use low tones when speaking and refrain from sudden movements. If in a group, maintain quiet conversations and avoid crowding around an animal.

4. Adhere to Park Guidelines

Each park or wildlife area may have specific rules regarding wildlife viewing. For instance, in Denali National Park, visitors are encouraged to use park buses for safe wildlife observation along the Denali Park Road. Transit bus tickets start at $30 per person.

5. Leave No Trace

Follow Leave No Trace principles by sticking to designated trails, packing out all trash, and avoiding damage to natural habitats. This practice helps preserve the environment for wildlife and future visitors.

6. Opt for Guided Tours

Consider joining a guided wildlife tour for expert insights and safer viewing experiences. Whale-watching tours in Juneau start at $120 per person, while bear-viewing tours in

Katmai National Park are around $950, including transportation. Guides are trained to ensure minimal impact on wildlife.

Chapter 8: Nome and the Arctic

When to Visit

The ideal time to visit Nome and the Arctic varies based on the experiences you're looking for, as each season brings its own unique attractions. From the Midnight Sun during summer to the Northern Lights in winter, Nome and the Arctic offer unforgettable adventures throughout the year. Here's a seasonal overview of what to expect.

Summer (June to August)

Summer is the most popular time to visit Nome and the Arctic, characterized by long daylight hours and mild temperatures ranging from 40°F to 60°F (4°C to 15°C). With nearly 24 hours of daylight thanks to the Midnight Sun, it's perfect for outdoor activities such as hiking, birdwatching, and gold panning.

Seasonal Highlights:

- **Birdwatching:** Nome becomes a prime destination for bird lovers, with migrating species like Arctic Warblers and Yellow Wagtails. The Safety Sound

Lagoon, located 20 miles (32 km) east of Nome, is particularly renowned for birding.

- **Gold Rush Legacy:** Experience gold panning along Nome's beaches, where the history of the gold rush is still alive. Equipment rentals start at $20 per day.

- **Fishing:** The Nome River and Snake River are excellent spots for salmon fishing. **Tips:** Make sure to book accommodations in advance, as summer is peak tourist season. Hotels in Nome, such as the Aurora Inn, start at around $200 per night.

Fall (September to October)

Fall in the Arctic is brief yet breathtaking, showcasing vibrant tundra colors and cooler temperatures ranging from 20°F to 40°F (-6°C to 4°C). This season sees fewer tourists, providing a quieter experience and the first glimpses of the Northern Lights.

Seasonal Highlights:

- **Tundra Colors:** The landscape transforms into vibrant reds, oranges, and yellows, making it an excellent time for photography.

- **Northern Lights:** By late September, the nights become dark enough to witness the aurora borealis. **Tips:** Dress in layers and bring waterproof clothing, as the weather can be unpredictable.

Winter (November to March)

Winter in Nome and the Arctic is a magical season marked by snow-covered landscapes and temperatures that can plunge to -40°F (-40°C). Despite the harsh cold, this time of year offers unique experiences such as dog sledding and aurora viewing.

Seasonal Highlights:

- **Northern Lights:** Winter is the prime season for seeing the aurora borealis, especially on clear nights away from city lights.

- **Iditarod Trail Sled Dog Race:** Nome serves as the finish line for this legendary race, held every March. Visitors can witness mushers and their teams completing the challenging 1,000-mile (1,609 km) journey.

- **Dog Sledding:** Local operators offer dog sledding tours starting at $150 per person. **Tips:** Pack heavy winter clothing, including insulated boots, gloves, and a warm parka. Round-trip flights to Nome from Anchorage start at $500.

Spring (April to May)

Spring in the Arctic is a transitional period marked by melting snow and temperatures ranging from 20°F to 40°F (-6°C to 4°C). Although it's less frequented by tourists, it's an excellent time to appreciate the region's serene beauty.

Seasonal Highlights:

- **Wildlife Viewing:** As the snow melts, caribou and musk oxen become more active.

- **Cultural Events:** Spring festivals in Nome celebrate the arrival of warmer weather and local traditions.

    Tips: Be prepared for muddy conditions as the snow begins to thaw.

Top Attractions

Nome and the Arctic region of Alaska present a distinctive combination of natural beauty, cultural heritage, and outdoor adventures. With a rich gold rush history and breathtaking landscapes, these destinations offer unforgettable experiences for travelers looking for something off the beaten path. Here are the top attractions to explore, along with practical tips for your visit.

1. Nome's Gold Rush Heritage

Nome is renowned for its gold rush history, allowing visitors to relive the excitement of that era.

- **Gold Panning:** Experience the thrill of gold panning along Nome's beaches, where many prospectors once struck it rich. Equipment rentals are available for about $20 per day, and guided tours start at $50.

- **Historic Sites:** Visit the Carrie M. McLain Memorial Museum to delve into Nome's gold rush history and learn about early settlers. Admission is $5 for adults.

- **Best Time to Visit:** The summer months (June to August) are perfect for outdoor activities, with temperatures ranging from 40°F to 60°F (4°C to 15°C).

2. Iditarod Trail Sled Dog Race Finish Line

Nome serves as the finish line for the famous Iditarod Trail Sled Dog Race, held every March.

- **What to Expect:** Witness mushers and their dog teams cross the finish line after a challenging 1,000-mile (1,609 km) journey from Anchorage. The city buzzes with celebrations, cultural events, and opportunities to meet the mushers.

- **Best Time to Visit:** March, when the race concludes. Be prepared for temperatures that can drop to -20°F (-29°C).

3. Northern Lights Viewing

The Arctic is one of the best locations globally to witness the aurora borealis.

- **Top Viewing Spots:**
    - **Nome:** Venture just outside the city to escape light pollution for the best views.
    - **Utqiaġvik (Barrow):** As the northernmost city in the U.S., it offers spectacular aurora displays during winter.

- **Best Time to Visit:** Late September to mid-April, with peak viewing during winter. Guided tours in Nome start at $100 per person and include transportation to prime viewing locations.

4. Arctic Wildlife Viewing

The Arctic is home to a diverse array of wildlife, including polar bears, musk oxen, and caribou.

- **Top Locations:**
    - **Nome's Countryside:** Drive along the Nome-Council Road or the Teller Road to spot musk oxen and caribou.
    - **Arctic National Wildlife Refuge:** This remote area is ideal for observing polar bears and migratory birds.
- **Best Time to Visit:** Summer (June to August) is excellent for birdwatching and general wildlife activity, while winter is best for polar bear sightings.

5. Bering Land Bridge National Preserve

This remote preserve near Nome offers insights into the region's ancient history and stunning landscapes.

- **Activities:**
    - Explore the Serpentine Hot Springs, a natural geothermal area surrounded by granite formations.
    - Hike or take a guided tour to learn about the area's significance as a migration route for early humans.
- **Best Time to Visit:** Summer, when the preserve is more accessible. Guided tours to the hot springs start at $300 per person, including transportation.

6. Utqiaġvik (Barrow)

Utqiaġvik, the northernmost city in the U.S., offers a unique blend of cultural and natural experiences.

- **Top Attractions:**
    - Visit the Iñupiat Heritage Center to learn about the traditions and culture of Alaska's Indigenous peoples. Admission is $10 for adults.

- Experience the Midnight Sun in summer or the Polar Night in winter.

- **Best Time to Visit:** Summer (June to August) for the Midnight Sun or winter (November to January) for the Polar Night.

7. Arctic Ocean Adventures

The Arctic Ocean provides unique opportunities for exploration.

- **Activities:**
  - Take a guided tour to dip your toes in the Arctic Ocean at Utqiaġvik or Nome.
  - Join a whale-watching tour to see bowhead whales and belugas, starting at $150 per person.

- **Best Time to Visit:** Summer, when the ocean is more accessible.

8. Cultural Festivals and Events

The Arctic region hosts several cultural events that celebrate Indigenous traditions and local heritage.

- **Notable Events:**

    - **King Island Native Community Festival (Nome):** Held in summer, this festival features traditional dances, crafts, and storytelling.

    - **Piuraagiaqta Festival (Utqiaġvik):** This spring festival marks the end of winter with games, music, and feasting.

- **Best Time to Visit:** Check local event calendars for specific dates.

Practical Tips for Visiting Nome and the Arctic

- **Transportation:** Nome is reachable by air from Anchorage, with round-trip flights starting at $500. Utqiaġvik also has air access, with flights starting at $600.

- **Accommodations:** Hotels in Nome, like the Aurora Inn, start at around $200 per night. In Utqiaġvik, options such as the Top of the World Hotel begin at $250 per night.

- **Weather:** Prepare for extreme weather, especially in winter, with insulated boots, gloves, and parkas.

Where to Eat and Stay

Nome, a remote yet lively town on Alaska's western coast, boasts a surprising array of dining and lodging options that cater to various budgets and preferences. Whether you're drawn to its gold rush history, wildlife, or cultural experiences, you'll find comfortable accommodations and satisfying meals to enhance your visit.

Where to Stay in Nome

1. Aurora Inn & Suites

- **Overview:** A modern and inviting choice, the Aurora Inn is one of the most popular places to stay in Nome. It features spacious rooms with amenities like complimentary Wi-Fi, a fitness center, and a business center.

- **Price Range:** Rooms typically cost between $200 and $250 per night.

- **Location:** Centrally located, within easy walking distance of restaurants and shops.

- **Best For:** Travelers seeking comfort and convenience.

2. Dredge No. 7 Inn

- **Overview:** This boutique inn exudes a cozy, home-like ambiance with themed rooms inspired by Nome's gold rush era. It's an excellent option for those wanting a unique lodging experience.

- **Price Range:** Rooms range from $150 to $200 per night.

- **Location:** Approximately 1 mile (1.6 km) from downtown Nome, providing a quieter atmosphere.

- **Best For:** History buffs and those looking for a personalized stay.

3. Airbnb and Vacation Rentals

- **Overview:** For budget-conscious travelers or those planning extended stays, Airbnb offers a variety of accommodations, including private rooms and entire homes. Prices vary based on the property.

- **Price Range:** Typically between $100 and $200 per night.

- **Best For:** Families, groups, or visitors desiring a more local experience.

4. Nome Nugget Inn

- **Overview:** Known as the oldest hotel in Nome, the Nome Nugget Inn offers rustic charm with basic amenities. It's a budget-friendly choice for those prioritizing location over luxury.
- **Price Range:** Rooms start at $120 to $150 per night.
- **Location:** Situated in the heart of Nome, close to the beach and local attractions.
- **Best For:** Budget travelers and history enthusiasts.

Where to Eat in Nome

1. Milano's Pizzeria

- **Overview:** A local favorite, Milano's serves delicious pizzas, pasta, and Italian-American dishes. The generous portions and casual atmosphere make it a great spot for families.
- **Price Range:** Meals range from $15 to $25.

- **Location:** Located in downtown Nome, within walking distance of most hotels.

- **Best For:** Families and casual dining.

2. Bering Sea Bar & Grill

- **Overview:** This restaurant offers a blend of American and seafood dishes, featuring fresh halibut and salmon. It's perfect for a hearty meal after a day of exploration.

- **Price Range:** Meals typically cost between $20 and $40.

- **Location:** Near the Nome waterfront.

- **Best For:** Seafood lovers and those looking for a lively dining atmosphere.

3. Polar Café

- **Overview:** A cozy diner-style café serving breakfast, lunch, and dinner. Popular items include reindeer sausage, burgers, and hearty breakfasts.

- **Price Range:** Meals are priced between $10 and $20.

- **Location:** Centrally located in Nome, near the Aurora Inn.
- **Best For:** Budget-friendly meals with a local vibe.

4. Airport Pizza

- **Overview:** Famous for its unique delivery service by plane to remote villages, Airport Pizza is a must-try in Nome. The menu features pizzas, sandwiches, and salads.
- **Price Range:** Meals range from $15 to $30.
- **Location:** Close to Nome Airport, about 2 miles (3.2 km) from downtown.
- **Best For:** Travelers seeking a quirky dining experience.

5. Nome Subway

- **Overview:** For a quick and affordable meal, Nome's Subway offers a familiar menu of sandwiches and salads.
- **Price Range:** Meals typically cost between $8 and $15.

- **Location:** Situated in downtown Nome.
- **Best For:** Budget-conscious travelers or those in a hurry.

Tips for Dining and Lodging in Nome

- **Book Early:** Accommodations in Nome are limited and fill up quickly, especially during events like the Iditarod finish in March.
- **Try Local Delicacies:** Don't miss the opportunity to sample reindeer sausage or fresh seafood at local restaurants.
- **Transportation:** Most hotels and restaurants are within walking distance in downtown Nome, but taxis are available for locations further out.

Chapter 9: Off-the-Grid Escapes and Outdoor Adventures

Backcountry Hiking and Camping

Alaska's backcountry provides some of the most remote and stunning wilderness experiences on the planet. With its expansive landscapes, rugged terrain, and rich wildlife, it is a true paradise for adventurers. However, hiking and camping in Alaska's backcountry necessitate meticulous planning, preparation, and respect for the natural environment.

Recommended Locations

1. Denali National Park

- **Overview:** Denali's backcountry is segmented into units, and permits are necessary for overnight stays. The park offers limitless opportunities for off-trail hiking, featuring highlights such as the Teklanika River and Polychrome Pass.

- **Access:** The Denali Park Road allows access to various backcountry units, with transit buses starting at $30 per person.

- **Tips:** Be ready for river crossings and ensure you carry bear spray.

2. Lake Clark National Park

- **Overview:** Renowned for its pristine lakes and rugged mountain scenery, Lake Clark provides remote camping options near Telaquana Lake or Turquoise Lake.

- **Access:** The park is reachable only by air taxi from Anchorage or Homer, with flights starting at $300 per person.

- **Tips:** Bring a water filter, as natural water sources may contain sediment.

3. Wrangell-St. Elias National Park

- **Overview:** As the largest national park in the U.S., Wrangell-St. Elias boasts glaciers, alpine meadows, and remote valleys. Notable areas include the Root Glacier and the Nabesna Road region.

- **Access:** You can drive to McCarthy or the Nabesna Road. Guided trips are available, starting at $200 per day.

- **Tips:** Use crampons for glacier hikes and adhere to Leave No Trace principles.

Safety Tips

1. Wildlife Awareness

- Alaska is home to bears, so carry bear spray (approximately $40 - $50) and store food in bear-resistant containers, which can be rented for $5 - $10 per day. Make noise while hiking to avoid startling wildlife.

2. Navigation

- Cell phone service is limited in the backcountry. Carry a topographic map, compass, and GPS device, and practice your orienteering skills before your trip.

3. Weather Preparedness

- The weather in Alaska can be unpredictable. Pack layers, including a waterproof jacket and insulated clothing. Summer temperatures can vary from 30°F to 70°F (-1°C to 21°C).

4. Water Safety

- Always treat water sources by boiling, filtering, or using purification tablets. Avoid drinking directly from glacial streams, as they may contain sediment.

5. Emergency Planning

- Leave your itinerary with a trusted person. Consider renting a satellite phone or a personal locator beacon for emergencies.

Kayaking, Fishing, and Dog Sledding

Alaska's expansive wilderness offers fantastic opportunities for outdoor enthusiasts, with activities like kayaking, fishing, and dog sledding being among the most popular. Whether you're new to these adventures or a seasoned pro, these experiences provide unforgettable ways to immerse yourself in Alaska's stunning natural scenery.

Kayaking

Kayaking in Alaska allows you to navigate pristine waters while getting close to glaciers and wildlife.

- **Best Locations:**

    o **Kenai Fjords National Park (Seward):** Paddle alongside majestic glaciers while spotting sea otters, seals, and puffins. Guided half-day tours start at $150 per person.

    o **Prince William Sound (Whittier):** Renowned for its calm waters, this area is perfect for beginners. Full-day tours begin at $200 per person.

- **Tips:** Beginners should opt for guided tours to ensure safety and proper navigation. Dress in layers and wear waterproof gear, as temperatures can be cool on the water.

Fishing

Alaska is a premier fishing destination, offering chances to catch salmon, halibut, and trout.

- **Best Locations:**
  - **Homer:** Known as the "Halibut Fishing Capital of the World," Homer features charters starting at $250 per person for half-day trips.
  - **Kenai River:** Famous for its king salmon runs, the Kenai River is a favorite among anglers. Guided fishing trips typically start at $200 per person.
- **Tips:** Obtain a fishing license online or at local stores (starting at $15 for a one-day license). Bring waterproof boots and layered clothing for comfort.

Dog Sledding

Dog sledding is a quintessential Alaskan adventure available throughout the year.

- **Best Locations:**
  - **Girdwood:** Helicopter tours to glacier dog camps start at $600 per person, allowing you to mush on snow even in summer.

- ○ **Fairbanks:** Winter dog sledding tours begin at $150 per person and often include opportunities to meet the dogs and learn the basics of mushing.

- **Tips:** Dress warmly, especially during winter months, with insulated boots and gloves. Make sure to book your tours in advance, as they fill up quickly during peak seasons.

Staying Safe in the Wilderness

Venturing into Alaska's wilderness is a remarkable experience, but it requires careful preparation and caution to ensure your safety.

Navigation

Alaska's expansive landscapes can be confusing, particularly in remote regions. Always bring along a detailed topographic map and a compass, and make sure you know how to use them effectively. While GPS devices can be useful, they should not replace traditional navigation methods, as batteries may fail in cold conditions. For longer trips, consider renting a satellite phone or personal locator beacon (PLB), typically costing around $15 - $20 per day. Be aware that cell service is often limited in wilderness areas, so do not rely solely on your phone.

Wildlife Encounters

Alaska is home to various large animals, including bears and moose. To minimize the risk of encounters, make noise while hiking by clapping or speaking, especially in dense brush or near water sources. Always carry bear spray (approximately $40 - $50) and keep it readily accessible. If you do come across a bear, remain calm, back away slowly, and avoid running. Store food in bear-resistant containers, which can often be rented for $5 - $10 per day at many parks.

Emergency Preparedness

The weather in Alaska can change unexpectedly. Pack in layers, including a waterproof jacket, and always carry extra food, water, and a first-aid kit. If you're hiking in remote areas, inform someone of your itinerary and your expected return time. In the event of an emergency, stay in one location to make it easier for rescuers to locate you.

Chapter 10: Practical Travel Tips and Resources

Packing for Alaska

Packing for Alaska requires thoughtful preparation due to its unpredictable weather and variety of activities. Whether you plan to hike, view wildlife, or explore urban areas, having the right gear is crucial.

Clothing Essentials

- **Layered Clothing:** Since Alaska's weather can change rapidly, it's important to pack in layers. Start with moisture-wicking base layers (approximately $30 - $60), add insulating mid-layers like fleece or down jackets (ranging from $50 - $150), and top it off with a waterproof outer layer (costing between $100 - $200).

- **Footwear:** Waterproof hiking boots (priced at $100 - $200) are essential for trails, while comfortable walking shoes are best for city exploration. Don't forget to pack extra socks, preferably made of wool or synthetic materials, to keep your feet dry.

- **Accessories:** Include a warm hat, gloves, and a neck gaiter for cooler days. Sunglasses and sunscreen are necessary year-round, especially in snowy or glacial environments.

Seasonal Additions

- **Summer (June–August):** Lightweight rain gear is crucial, as summer showers are frequent. In areas with heavy mosquito populations, bug spray and a bug net (costing $10 - $20) are advisable.

- **Winter (November–March):** Insulated boots, thermal gloves, and a heavy parka (ranging from $150 - $300) are essential for sub-zero temperatures.

Activity-Specific Gear

- **Hiking:** Bring a daypack (costing $30 - $70), trekking poles (priced at $30 - $80), and a reusable water bottle.

- **Wildlife Viewing:** Binoculars (ranging from $50 - $200) and a camera with a zoom lens are important for safely observing wildlife from a distance.

- **Camping:** Pack a cold-weather-rated sleeping bag, a portable stove, and bear-resistant food containers (available for rent at $5 - $10 per day).

Practical Tips

- **Pack Light:** Many accommodations provide laundry facilities, allowing you to wash clothes during your trip.

- **Weather Preparedness:** Always check the weather forecast and pack accordingly. Even in summer, temperatures can drop to 40°F (4°C) in the evenings.

- **Organize Your Gear:** Utilize packing cubes to keep your items organized and easily accessible.

Flights, Ferries, and Road Trips

Navigating Alaska requires a variety of transportation options due to its expansive size and remote locations.

Whether you're flying between cities, cruising along the coast, or driving through scenic highways, understanding your choices will help ensure a smooth journey.

Flights

Flying is the quickest way to travel between Alaska's major cities and remote regions.

- **Major Airports:** Ted Stevens Anchorage International Airport and Fairbanks International Airport serve as the primary hubs for domestic and international flights. Smaller airports, such as Juneau and Nome, connect to regional destinations.

- **Bush Flights:** For access to remote areas like Denali, the Arctic, or small coastal towns, bush planes are essential. Airlines like Ravn Alaska and Alaska Seaplanes offer one-way flights starting at $150 - $300.

- **Tips:** Reserve your flights early, particularly during the summer months (June–August), when demand peaks. For breathtaking views, request a window seat on flights over glaciers or mountain ranges.

Ferries

The Alaska Marine Highway System (AMHS) provides a unique way to explore coastal towns and islands.

- **Routes:** Ferries connect cities like Juneau, Ketchikan, Sitka, and Whittier, along with smaller communities. The Inside Passage is a popular route known for its stunning views of glaciers and wildlife.

- **Costs:** Passenger fares start at $50 - $100, with additional charges for vehicles. Cabins are available for overnight journeys, beginning at $100.

- **Tips:** Book ferry trips several months in advance, especially for summer travel. Bring snacks and dress in layers, as temperatures on deck can be cool.

Road Trips

Driving is one of the best ways to experience Alaska's breathtaking landscapes, with well-maintained highways connecting key destinations.

- **Top Routes:**

- - **Seward Highway:** This 127-mile (204 km) stretch from Anchorage to Seward offers views of mountains, glaciers, and Turnagain Arm.
  - **Parks Highway:** A 360-mile (579 km) route linking Anchorage and Fairbanks, passing through Denali National Park.
  - **Dalton Highway:** A rugged 414-mile (666 km) road leading to the Arctic Circle, best suited for experienced drivers with 4WD vehicles.
- **Car Rentals:** Rental rates in Anchorage or Fairbanks start at $50 - $100 per day. If you plan to travel to remote areas, verify that your rental agreement allows for travel on gravel roads.
- **Tips:** Gas stations can be infrequent in remote regions, so fill up whenever you can. Always carry a spare tire and emergency supplies.

Navigating Remote Areas

- **Weather:** Be ready for abrupt weather changes, particularly in mountainous or coastal areas.

- **Maps:** Since cell service may be limited in many locations, bring a physical map or download offline maps.

- **Local Advice:** Consult with visitor centers or locals for information on road conditions and travel recommendations.

Budgeting and Planning Your Trip

Planning a trip to Alaska requires thoughtful budgeting, as the state's remote nature and distinctive experiences can lead to higher expenses. However, with strategic planning and cost-saving approaches, you can enjoy the beauty of Alaska without breaking the bank.

Transportation Costs

Flights to Alaska often represent one of the largest expenses. Round-trip tickets from major U.S. cities to Anchorage or Fairbanks generally range from $400 to $800, depending on the time of year. To save money, book your flights 3 to 6 months in advance and consider traveling during the shoulder seasons (May or September) when fares tend to be lower. For accessing remote areas,

Alaska Airlines offers affordable regional flights, and the Alaska Marine Highway ferries provide economical transportation between coastal towns, with fares starting at $50 per person.

Accommodations

Lodging options in Alaska vary widely, from budget hostels ($30 - $50 per night) to mid-range hotels ($150 - $300 per night) and luxury lodges ($400 and up per night). To cut costs, consider camping in state or national parks, where fees range from $10 to $30 per night. Booking your accommodations well in advance, particularly during the summer, will help secure better rates and availability.

Activities and Tours

Alaska's signature activities—such as glacier cruises, wildlife tours, and dog sledding—can be expensive. For example, glacier cruises in Kenai Fjords National Park start at $150 per person, while dog sledding tours can range from $150 to $600. To save money, focus on the activities that are most important to you and look for discounts by booking directly with local operators. There are also several free or low-cost options available, including hiking trails, visiting cultural centers, and scenic drives like the Seward Highway.

Food and Dining

Dining in Alaska can be costly, with meals at mid-range restaurants typically priced between $15 and $30 per person. To save on food expenses, consider shopping at local grocery stores and preparing your own meals, especially if you have access to kitchen facilities in your accommodations.

Conclusion

Alaska is more than just a travel destination; it's an unforgettable experience that lingers in your memory long after your journey concludes. With its majestic mountains, vast glaciers, vibrant wildlife, and rich cultural heritage, Alaska offers a sense of wonder that few places on Earth can rival. Whether you've wandered through the lively streets of Anchorage, admired the Northern Lights in Fairbanks, or explored the remote wilderness of Denali, every moment in Alaska serves as a testament to the beauty and power of nature.

Reflecting on your trip, you'll come to understand that Alaska is not solely about the locations you visit, but the memories you forge. It's the excitement of spotting a grizzly bear in its natural habitat, the tranquility of paddling through glacial waters, and the warmth of engaging with locals who call this rugged terrain home. Alaska invites you to step outside your comfort zone, embrace the unexpected, and cherish the simplicity of life in its most authentic form.

This guide has been crafted to help you navigate Alaska's expansive landscapes, plan unforgettable adventures, and make the most of your time in this remarkable state. Yet, the true enchantment of Alaska lies in its ability to astonish you—whether through a spontaneous wildlife encounter, a stunning view just around the corner, or a quiet moment of reflection beneath the midnight sun.

As you finish this guide, keep in mind that Alaska is a place meant to be revisited time and again. Its beauty is eternal, its spirit unwavering, and its allure irresistible. Safe travels, and may your Alaskan adventure continue to inspire you for years to come.

Bonus

Congratulations on acquiring the *Alaska Travel Guide 2025*! As a token of appreciation, I'm thrilled to offer you some exclusive bonuses to enrich your Alaskan adventure and make it truly unforgettable.

Inside your guide, you'll find meticulously designed itineraries for 3-day, 7-day, and 14-day trips, each tailored to accommodate various travel styles and interests.

Additionally, to elevate your culinary experience, the guide features a selection of must-try Alaskan dishes along with recommendations on where to sample them, ensuring you can enjoy the state's distinctive flavors. Enjoy your journey!

Detailed Maps of Key Regions

Navigating the vast and varied landscapes of Alaska can be a challenge, but having detailed maps of the state's key regions is crucial for effective planning and exploration. Whether you're driving along picturesque highways, hiking in remote areas, or cruising through coastal waters, maps are invaluable for identifying major attractions, planning your routes, and estimating travel times. Here's how to utilize them effectively.

Southeast Alaska

Maps of Southeast Alaska, often referred to as the Inside Passage, showcase ferry routes, island communities, and notable attractions. The Alaska Marine Highway System map is especially helpful for organizing ferry trips between towns like Juneau, Sitka, and Ketchikan. Distances between locations are frequently listed in nautical miles, with ferry rides typically lasting between 3 to 10 hours, depending on the specific route. Juneau maps will direct you to landmarks such as Mendenhall Glacier (located 12 miles/19 km from downtown) and various hiking trails in Tongass National Forest.

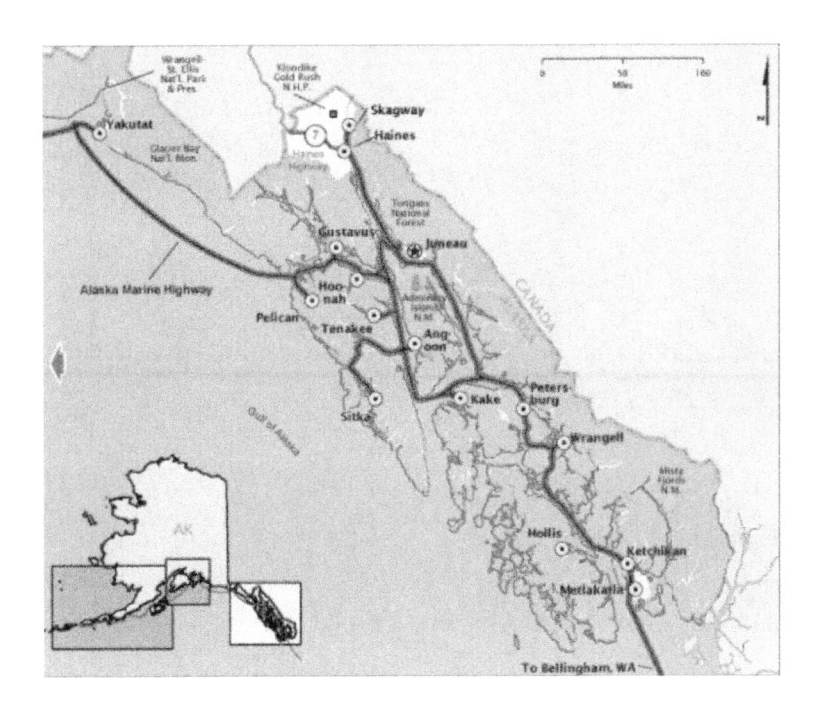

Southcentral Alaska

Maps of Southcentral Alaska emphasize key roadways such as the Seward Highway and Glenn Highway, linking Anchorage to popular destinations like Seward (127 miles/204 km) and Valdez (305 miles/491 km). Additionally, these maps showcase attractions like Kenai

Fjords National Park, Prince William Sound, and the Chugach Mountains.

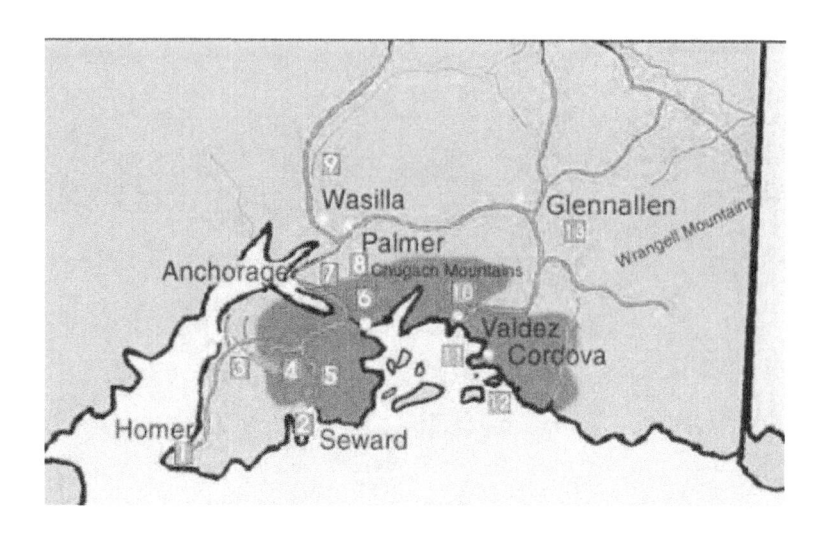

Interior Alaska

Maps of Interior Alaska are crucial for discovering the expansive wilderness and isolated towns. The Parks Highway map links Anchorage to Fairbanks (360 miles/579 km) and traverses Denali National Park. Maps specific to Denali are especially useful for navigating the park's shuttle bus system and hiking paths. In Fairbanks, maps can help you locate attractions such as Chena Hot Springs (60 miles/97 km from downtown) and prime spots for viewing the aurora.

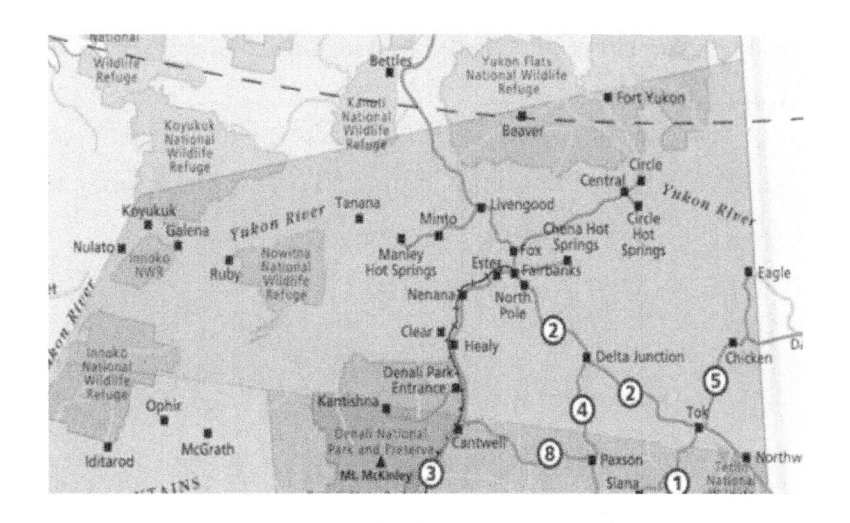

Itineraries for Every Traveler (3-Day, 7-Day, and 14-Day Plans)

Organizing a trip to Alaska can be daunting given its size and variety of attractions. Whether you have a few days or up to two weeks, these sample itineraries will assist you in maximizing your experience. Each itinerary is tailored to different travel preferences, ranging from nature enthusiasts to adventure lovers, and includes useful details to help ensure a seamless journey.

3-Day Itinerary: A Taste of Alaska's Natural Beauty and Culture

Ideal for: Those with limited time who wish to experience Alaska's scenic landscapes and cultural heritage.

Day 1: Anchorage

- **Morning:** Arrive in Anchorage and rent a car (starting at $50/day). Visit the Anchorage Museum ($20/adult) to discover Alaska's history and indigenous cultures.

- **Afternoon:** Enjoy a walk or bike ride along the Tony Knowles Coastal Trail (11 miles/17.7 km) for breathtaking views of Cook Inlet and the Chugach Mountains.

- **Evening:** Dine at 49th State Brewing Co., where dishes like halibut tacos range from $20 to $30. Stay overnight in Anchorage (budget hotels starting at $120/night).

Day 2: Seward and Kenai Fjords National Park

- **Morning:** Drive the picturesque Seward Highway (127 miles/204 km, approximately 2.5 hours). Stop at Beluga Point and Turnagain Pass for photo opportunities.

- **Afternoon:** Embark on a Kenai Fjords glacier and wildlife cruise ($150 - $200/person) to spot whales, sea lions, and observe calving glaciers.

- **Evening:** Stroll around Seward's harbor and dine at Ray's Waterfront (entrees priced between $25 and $40). Spend the night in Seward.

Day 3: Exit Glacier and Return to Anchorage

- **Morning:** Hike the Exit Glacier Trail (an easy 1.8 miles/2.9 km round trip) or opt for the more challenging Harding Icefield Trail (8.2 miles/13.2 km round trip).

- **Afternoon:** Head back to Anchorage, stopping at the Alaska Wildlife Conservation Center ($17/adult) to see bears, moose, and bison.

- **Evening:** Depart from Anchorage.

7-Day Itinerary: National Parks and Scenic Drives

Ideal for: Travelers eager to explore Alaska's iconic parks and landscapes.

Day 1: Anchorage

- Arrive, explore the city, and stay overnight in Anchorage.

Day 2: Denali National Park

- **Morning:** Drive the Parks Highway (240 miles/386 km, about 4.5 hours) to Denali.

- **Afternoon:** Visit the Denali Visitor Center and hike the Horseshoe Lake Trail (2 miles/3.2 km). Overnight near the park (lodges from $200/night).

Day 3: Denali National Park

- Take a Denali Transit Bus to Mile 43 (Teklanika River, $30/person) for wildlife viewing and stunning mountain views.

Day 4: Talkeetna

- Drive to Talkeetna (152 miles/244 km, roughly 2.5 hours). Experience a flightseeing tour over Denali, including a glacier landing ($300 - $400/person). Overnight in Talkeetna.

Day 5: Seward

- Drive to Seward (238 miles/383 km, about 5 hours), stopping at scenic viewpoints along the way. Overnight in Seward.

Day 6: Kenai Fjords National Park

- Enjoy a glacier and wildlife cruise or kayak in Resurrection Bay. Visit the Alaska SeaLife Center ($30/adult).

Day 7: Return to Anchorage

- Drive back to Anchorage and depart.

14-Day Itinerary: Comprehensive Alaska Adventure

Ideal for: Those with ample time to explore multiple regions and off-the-beaten-path destinations.

Days 1–2: Anchorage and Girdwood

- Discover Anchorage and take a day trip to Girdwood (40 miles/64 km). Ride the Alyeska Tram ($35/adult) for panoramic views.

Days 3–5: Denali National Park

- Travel to Denali and spend three days exploring the park, including a guided rafting trip on the Nenana River ($100 - $150/person).

Days 6–7: Fairbanks

- Drive to Fairbanks (121 miles/195 km). Visit Chena Hot Springs ($15/adult) and the University of Alaska Museum of the North ($16/adult).

Days 8–9: Wrangell-St. Elias National Park

- Head to McCarthy (311 miles/500 km, about 7 hours). Explore the Kennecott Mines and participate in a glacier hike ($100 - $150/person).

Days 10–12: Seward and Kenai Fjords

- Return to Southcentral Alaska and spend three days in Seward, including a hike on the Harding Icefield Trail and a wildlife cruise.

Days 13–14: Homer

- Drive to Homer (170 miles/274 km, around 4 hours). Explore Homer Spit, go halibut fishing, or take a bear-viewing tour to Katmai National Park ($600 - $800/person).

12 Must-Try Alaskan Dishes and Where to Find Them

Alaska's culinary landscape is as distinctive as its scenery, featuring fresh seafood, wild game, and traditional Native Alaskan fare. Here are 12 iconic Alaskan dishes, their cultural significance, and recommendations on where to sample them during your trip.

1. **Wild Alaskan Salmon**

   A cornerstone of Alaskan cuisine, salmon is renowned for its rich flavor and versatility. Enjoy it grilled, smoked, or in chowder. Ray's Waterfront in Seward offers a variety of fresh salmon dishes, with entrees priced around $30 - $40.

2. **King Crab**

   Alaskan king crab is celebrated for its sweet and tender meat. A visit to Tracy's King Crab Shack in

Juneau is essential, where you can indulge in crab legs and bisque for $20 - $50.

3. **Halibut**

    Another local favorite, halibut is often enjoyed as fish and chips or grilled. The Cookery in Seward serves halibut entrees for $25 - $40.

4. **Reindeer Sausage**

    A beloved street food, reindeer sausage is a savory delight. You can find it at Anchorage's Downtown Market, where vendors sell it for $6 - $10.

5. **Alaskan Oysters**

    Known for their clean, briny taste, Alaskan oysters are a true delicacy. Homer Spit Oyster Bar in Homer serves fresh oysters for $2 - $3 each.

6. **Moose Stew**

    A hearty dish often prepared with root vegetables, moose stew is a comforting traditional meal. Try it at 49th State Brewing Co. in Anchorage, with prices around $15 - $20.

7. **Bannock**

    This traditional Native Alaskan fry bread is typically served with jam or honey. You can sample it at the Alaska Native Heritage Center in Anchorage during cultural events.

8. **Birch Syrup Treats**

    Made from the sap of birch trees, this syrup is featured in candies and baked goods. Alaska Birch Syrup & Wild Harvest Products in Talkeetna offers samples and treats starting at $5.

9. **Eskimo Ice Cream (Akutaq)**

    A traditional dish made from whipped fat, berries, and fish, Akutaq offers a unique cultural experience. It's best enjoyed at community events in Arctic villages like Utqiaġvik.

10. **Alaskan Blueberries**

    Wild blueberries are often used in pies, jams, and syrups. The Bake Shop in Girdwood serves delicious blueberry pie for about $6 per slice.

11. **Caribou Burger**

Lean and flavorful, caribou meat is commonly served as burgers. Arctic Roadrunner in Anchorage features caribou burgers priced at $12 - $15.

12. **Muktuk**

A traditional Inuit dish made from whale skin and blubber, muktuk is a cultural delicacy best experienced at festivals or cultural events in Arctic communities.

About the Author

Wyatt Caleb is an experienced travel writer and adventurer with a deep enthusiasm for discovering some of the world's most stunning locations. With over a decade of experience, he specializes in creating practical and engaging travel guides that empower travelers to explore new destinations with confidence. His skills include uncovering hidden treasures, sharing valuable insider tips, and designing itineraries that accommodate various travel preferences.

A lifelong wanderer, Wyatt's passion for travel ignited with road trips across the United States, eventually taking him to remote areas around the globe. He believes that travel should be enriching, accessible, and enjoyable, which is why his guides emphasize a blend of cultural immersion, outdoor activities, and practical advice.

Outside of writing, Wyatt loves hiking, photography, and engaging with locals to gain insights into their traditions and lifestyles. His friendly approach and meticulous attention to detail have made his guides a reliable resource for travelers in search of memorable experiences.